Options for Tax Reform

Brookings Dialogues on Public Policy

*The presentations and discussions at Brookings conferences and seminars
often deserve wide circulation as contributions to public understanding
of issues of national importance. The Brookings Dialogues on Public Policy
series is intended to make such statements and commentary available
to a broad and general audience, usually in summary form. The series
supplements the Institution's research publications by reflecting
the contrasting, often lively, and sometimes conflicting views of elected
and appointed government officials, other leaders in public and private life,
and scholars. In keeping with their origin and purpose, the Dialogues
are not subjected to the formal review procedures established for the
Institution's research publications. Brookings publishes them in the belief
that they are worthy of public consideration but does not assume
responsibility for their accuracy or objectivity. And, as in all Brookings
publications, the judgments, conclusions, and recommendations
presented in the Dialogues should not be ascribed to the trustees, officers,
or other staff members of the Brookings Institution.*

Options for Tax Reform

Papers by RICHARD GOODE

SLADE GORTON

MICHAEL J. GRAETZ

RICHARD A. GEPHARDT

GORDON D. HENDERSON

HENRY J. AARON & HARVEY GALPER

*presented at a conference at the Brookings Institution
on April 23–24, 1984*

Edited by JOSEPH A. PECHMAN

THE BROOKINGS INSTITUTION
Washington, D.C.

THE FINANCIAL EXECUTIVES
RESEARCH FOUNDATION
Morristown, N.J.

About Brookings

THE BROOKINGS INSTITUTION is a private nonprofit organization devoted to research, education, and publication in economics, government, foreign policy, and the social sciences generally. Its principal purpose is to bring knowledge to bear on the current and emerging public policy problems facing the American people. In its research, Brookings functions as an independent analyst and critic, committed to publishing its findings for the information of the public. In its conferences and other activities, it serves as a bridge between scholarship and public policy, bringing new knowledge to the attention of decisionmakers and affording scholars a better insight into policy issues. Its activities are carried out through three research programs (Economic Studies, Governmental Studies, Foreign Policy Studies), an Advanced Study Program, a Publications Program, and a Social Science Computation Center.

The Institution was incorporated in 1927 to merge the Institute for Government Research, founded in 1916 as the first private organization devoted to public policy issues at the national level; the Institute of Economics, established in 1922 to study economic problems; and the Robert Brookings Graduate School of Economics and Government, organized in 1924 as a pioneering experiment in training for public service. The consolidated institution was named in honor of Robert Somers Brookings (1850–1932), a St. Louis businessman whose leadership shaped the earlier organizations.

Brookings is financed largely by endowment and by the support of philanthropic foundations, corporations, and private individuals. Its funds are devoted to carrying out its own research and educational activities. It also undertakes some unclassified government contract studies, reserving the right to publish its findings.

A Board of Trustees is responsible for general supervision of the Institution, approval of fields of investigation, and safeguarding the independence of the Institution's work. The President is the chief administrative officer, responsible for formulating and coordinating policies, recommending projects, approving publications, and selecting the staff.

About FERF

THE FINANCIAL EXECUTIVES RESEARCH FOUNDATION is the research arm of the Financial Executives Institute. The basic objective of the foundation is to sponsor fundamental research and publish authoritative material in the field of business management, with particular emphasis on the principles and practices of financial management and its evolving role in the management of business.

The Financial Executives Institute mission is to maintain a position of national leadership on issues affecting corporate financial management and to provide services that will best meet the professional needs of its members. The institute comprises 12,500 individual members, who function at the policymaking level of approximately 6,000 businesses in the United States and Canada. Its objectives are to provide and stimulate exposure to different points of view, develop a superior body of knowledge of advanced financial management, and serve as an effective spokesman in and for the business community.

Preface

THE PUBLIC and the Congress are showing renewed interest in reforms to simplify the federal income tax. Public opinion polls indicate that the income tax, once regarded as the fairest tax, is now the least popular in the federal system. In part, this opinion reflects the growing complexity of the income tax code and the tax return. It also reflects the view that tax preferences are permitting many people to avoid their fair share of the tax burden.

The idea of tax reform has also gained momentum from the explosion of the federal deficit since 1981 and the resulting need to increase federal revenue. Although most tax reform proposals are intended as a more equitable way of yielding approximately the same revenue as the present tax system, they can also be viewed as a fairer means to raise additional revenue.

This book reports on the proceedings of a conference of experts representing various shades of opinion who were invited to sort out the issues and to evaluate the various tax reform proposals. The conference, held on April 23–24, 1984, was organized by the Brookings Institution's Advanced Study Program, which is under the direction of A. Lee Fritschler, and the Financial Executives Research Foundation. The participants consisted of former and present officials of the Internal Revenue Service and the Treasury Department, financial executives of major U.S. corporations, and leading tax economists and tax lawyers. The opinions expressed by the participants reflect their own views and not those of the organizations with which they are affiliated.

Julia Sternberg helped organize the conference, Julia Leighton provided research assistance, and Carolyn Rutsch checked references. Susan Woollen typed parts of the manuscript, Gregg Forte and James Schneider edited it, and Nancy Snyder proofread it.

The Brookings Institution is grateful to the Financial Executives Research Foundation for their financial support of the project. We hope that this publication will be useful to the public and policymakers alike in the forthcoming discussions of tax policy.

BRUCE K. MACLAURY
President

Contents

ix

Introduction

JOSEPH A. PECHMAN

THE INDIVIDUAL INCOME TAX has been the backbone of the federal revenue system since the beginning of World War II, when exemptions were greatly reduced and most income recipients became subject to tax. Despite increases in exemptions and reductions in the marginal tax rates, the tax has produced more than 40 percent of federal revenues since then. In fiscal year 1985 the individual income tax will yield about $330 billion, or 44 percent of federal receipts.

By contrast, the corporation income tax has been declining in importance for the last three decades. In fiscal 1955 it produced 27 percent of federal receipts; in 1985 only about 10 percent. The corporation income tax is needed as a safeguard against wholesale avoidance of the individual income tax through the accumulation of retained earnings by corporations. This safeguard has been eroding as new corporate tax preferences have been introduced, allowances for capital investment have been liberalized, and interest payments on corporate debt have remained fully deductible. Nevertheless, the individual and corporation income taxes together still account for more than half of federal receipts.

Despite the heavy reliance placed on them, the income taxes have been under attack for many years. Some believe that they are unfair because they permit many people to escape their fair share of the tax burden. Others believe that they reduce incentives to work, save, and invest and therefore retard economic growth. Everybody believes that the taxes are unnecessarily complicated, distort economic behavior, and impose heavy costs on taxpayers and tax administrators alike.

Criticism of the income tax structure is not a new development. The Tax Reform Act of 1969 was passed in large measure because former Secretary of the Treasury Joseph J. Barr revealed that 154 taxpayers with incomes above $200,000 had not paid any taxes in 1967. Every president in recent memory has tried to improve the

I am grateful to Julia Leighton for assistance in the preparation of this chapter.

income tax system, yet taxes have become more complicated with the passage of each revenue act. The value of tax expenditures, a term that is meant to convey the idea that departures from the normal income tax structure are really substitutes for direct outlays by the federal government, now exceeds $350 billion and is rising in relation to actual tax collections.

Advocates of tax reform fall into two groups: those who believe that the income taxes are the fairest method of taxation seek to improve them; others who believe that consumption is a fairer basis of taxation than income argue for replacement of the income taxes by a graduated consumption tax. Both groups believe that the numerous tax preferences which have crept into the tax laws have produced great inequities and economic inefficiencies. A comprehensive tax base is thus regarded as a major ingredient of reform by all tax reformers; they disagree over the important issue of whether capital income should be taxed if it is not consumed.

Another strand of opinion in the current debate over tax policy derives from the obvious need for additional revenues in the years immediately ahead. Current estimates suggest that, unless substantial deficit-reducing measures are enacted soon, the federal deficit will remain above 5 percent of the gross national product for years to come. It is generally agreed that tax increases will be necessary to help reduce or eliminate this deficit. Many who support the income tax system fear that base broadening alone will not bring the deficits down because powerful political groups will be able to forestall significant tax reform. The only alternative, they believe, is to introduce a national sales tax or value-added tax to raise the additional revenue.

The papers and discussions presented in this volume cover these issues in some detail.[1] The first paper, by Richard Goode, discusses how the present state of affairs developed and draws lessons from this experience. This is followed by Michael J. Graetz's analysis of the shortcomings of the income taxes and methods to improve them. The last two papers discuss alternatives to the income taxes. Gordon D. Henderson is skeptical of the political acceptability of comprehensive tax reform and suggests that the federal government may have to turn to excise taxes on energy or to a value-added tax to raise the revenue needed to eliminate the deficit. Henry J. Aaron and Harvey Galper propose the substitution of a graduated tax on consumption and gifts and bequests for the

---

1. The papers in this volume do not reflect the provisions of the Deficit Reduction Act of 1984, which was passed after this conference was held.

individual income tax and a tax on cash flows for the corporation income tax. The conference also had the benefit of addresses by Senator Slade Gorton of Washington and Congressman Richard A. Gephardt of Missouri, the former on the practical difficulties of reforming the income taxes and the latter on the Bradley-Gephardt Fair Tax Act of 1983.

*How we got
where we are*

According to a public opinion poll published by the Advisory Commission on Intergovernmental Relations in 1983, a majority of adults in the United States favors progressive taxation but is dissatisfied with the present income tax. Richard Goode points out that many of the perceived inequities and inefficiencies have been in existence for a long time. For example, the personal deductions (for interest paid; state and local income, sales, and property taxes; medical expenses; and charitable contributions) were either part of the income tax when it was first enacted or were introduced more than forty years ago; social security payments were exempt from tax from the beginning of the social security system in the 1930s and have become subject to tax only for those with high other incomes beginning in 1984; and capital gains have been subject to preferential rates since 1921. But new preferences continue to be added and their use has become more widespread.

Goode attributes the present unpopularity of the income tax to three factors. First, the rapid increase in the number of tax expenditures and in the degree to which they are used has reduced the equity and increased the complexity of the tax system. These provisions benefit particular taxpayer groups, industries, and business firms, and many are considered unjustified and unfair. Second, the recent inflation pushed people into higher tax brackets ("bracket creep"), resulting in significant increases in average and marginal tax rates even though the nominal tax rates remained unchanged between 1971 and 1981. Third, many economists believe that a graduated consumption tax is fairer and more economically efficient than an income tax, and they have thus helped damage the prestige of the income taxes. As a result of these developments, many people were receptive to the supply-side arguments that the income taxes were hurting economic incentives and supported the 23 percent reduction in individual income tax rates and the new tax preferences for saving and investment enacted in 1981.

The experience with the income taxes, particularly that of recent years, leads Goode to a number of lessons regarding attitudes toward the income tax and potential for tax reform. He believes that there is general approval of the idea of progressive taxation, but people are frustrated with the present system because it has become so complicated and unfair. He does not believe that there is a strong commitment among the people or the politicians to an alternative form of taxation. He places a good deal of the blame for the poor understanding of the economics of taxation on the tax experts who emphasize theoretical models that rely on unrealistic assumptions to measure the impact of taxation.

Goode believes that the growth of tax preferences calls for a stronger stance by Congress against special interest groups. Many of the present tax expenditures were enacted in response to complaints of some groups that they were being treated unfairly in comparison with others. Instead of eliminating old preferences, Congress merely adds to the list without assessing the impact of the changes on the equity of the income tax and the complexity of the system.

Despite the discouraging evidence of recent experience, Goode is optimistic about the possibilities of tax reform. The history of the income taxes contains examples of constructive tax changes as well as retrogressions. He expects that the incrementalist approach to changes in tax policy, that is, the enactment of small changes that move the system in the right direction, will be the most successful but concedes that something can be said for attacking deficiencies on a broad front in the hope of encouraging supporters of tax reform and defusing the opposition. Senator Gorton agreed with Goode that the forces against comprehensive tax reform are extremely powerful and warned that tax reformers would be unsuccessful if their program were to become too ambitious.

Reforming the income tax   Michael Graetz also believes that the income tax is the most appropriate form of taxation on ethical and revenue grounds and sets out to show how it can be improved so that it can remain the major source of federal revenue. He points out that the current income tax already contains a variety of preferences for retirement savings that provide a useful lifetime averaging effect and thus mitigate the natural income tax preference for present over future consumption. The major income tax problems of the 1980s, according to Graetz, are to cope with inflation and compliance.

Proposals for comprehensive income taxation routinely ignore the problem of inflation, which Graetz believes must be handled if the income tax is to survive. Unexpected and fluctuating rates of inflation affect the income tax in three ways. First, bracket creep causes average and marginal tax rates on real incomes to rise without any congressional action. This has increased the value of tax expenditures and the distorting effect of the tax structure. Congress dealt with this problem by introducing automatic indexation of individual income tax rates, exemptions, and standard deductions beginning in 1985.

Second, in computing net income during an inflation, amounts spent in an earlier year's dollars are offset against income received in a subsequent year's dollars, which are worth less. This distortion affects the measurement of capital gains and losses, depreciation allowances, accounting for inventories, and the treatment of debt. The result is that taxable incomes may be overstated or understated, with borrowers being favored over lenders. Many individuals and business firms reduce or even eliminate their tax liabilities through "tax arbitrage," which usually involves borrowing to obtain funds for tax-preferred investments or for investments that produce large immediate tax write-offs. The remedy for these practices is to deny interest deductions for funds borrowed for these purposes, but Congress has done so only for a few types of transactions, and it is difficult to enforce even these mild limitations.

Third, inflation magnifies dramatically the significance of income tax timing issues. High interest rates have raised the tax advantage of allocating deductions to earlier tax years and income to later years. The 1982 act required for the first time compounding of interest with respect to tax underpayments and for measurement of interest income on bonds originally issued at a discount. Many more such anomalies remain, and Graetz believes that the income tax should be restructured to eliminate them.

The current state of the corporation income tax is deplorable, according to Graetz, because Congress has reacted to the effect of inflation by liberalizing investment allowances without doing anything about the overtaxation of lenders and undertaxation of borrowers. To remedy this situation, Graetz suggests that assets and debt alike should be adjusted to reflect inflation, depreciation allowances should be modified to provide more uniform rates of taxation among and within industries, and the tax on distributed earnings should be phased out.

Graetz expresses concern about trends in tax compliance. He believes that noncompliance has been increasing and that reductions in tax rates will not necessarily improve compliance. Nor does he believe that the substitution of a consumption tax for the income tax will improve matters. The only solution, according to Graetz, is to address head on the structural issues of detection and punishment.

Congressman Gephardt explained the basic principles of the Fair Tax proposal he and New Jersey Democratic Senator Bill Bradley have introduced to improve the equity of the individual and corporation income taxes and to simplify compliance and administration. The proposal would broaden the tax base by eliminating numerous deductions and exclusions, equalizing the tax rates on capital gains and losses and ordinary income, and removing the distortions in the depreciation allowances. With the base thus broadened, the individual income tax rates would be reduced to a maximum of 30 percent, consisting of a normal tax of 14 percent and a surtax ranging from 12 to 16 percent. The normal tax would apply to taxable income and the surtax to adjusted gross income. In this way, the deductions are, in effect, eliminated for surtax purposes and the tax value of the remaining deductions would be limited to 14 percent in all tax brackets. The corporation income tax rate would be set at 30 percent. Gephardt pointed out that, while the Fair Tax would not solve the inflation problems that concern Graetz, the proposed reduction in the marginal tax rates and widening of the tax brackets would moderate the inflation effects.

The value-added tax

Gordon Henderson believes that the income tax seriously distorts incentives to save, particularly during periods of inflation. These distortive effects have been magnified by the numerous provisions which were designed to moderate the adverse consequences of the tax structure and of the fiscal and regulatory conditions in which business must operate. He considers a number of alternatives to the present tax system and finds them all wanting.

The comprehensive income tax proposals are designed to raise the revenues produced by the present tax system, but no more. Henderson believes that they would lose their appeal if it were necessary to increase the tax rates to provide significantly greater amounts of revenue. Moreover, he doubts that Congress will come to grips with the many difficult issues that must be resolved in order to achieve a truly comprehensive tax base (for example, the treatment of fringe benefits). He is also concerned that elimination of the mortgage interest deduction would reduce property values and elimination of the deduction for state and local taxes would benefit some regions of the country at the expense of others.

Henderson is attracted by the favorable impact that a graduated consumption tax would have on saving (see below), but he reasons that such a tax would create a number of serious problems. It would be difficult to distinguish between investment and consumption; the treatment of accumulated wealth might be too favorable; there would be difficult problems of transition; coordination with foreign tax systems would not be easy; and the tax rates on consumption would be too high if additional revenue would be required to reduce the deficits.

If cuts in spending and broadening of the present income tax base do not raise enough revenue to eliminate the deficit problem, Henderson would turn next to excise taxes on mineral extraction. He feels that the present state severance taxes create unfair regional differences within the country, and he suggests that the federal government preempt this area of taxation.

The final alternative, the value-added tax, is similar to a sales tax, except that it is collected as the goods move through the chain of production and distribution. The value-added tax does not discourage saving, it can be relatively simple, and it is believed to be relatively easy to enforce. However, it too has a number of drawbacks, according to Henderson. The value-added tax would reduce progressivity and have an inflationary impact when it is introduced. The rates would be high if the tax is to produce any significant amounts of revenue. The tax would be viewed as a one-time levy on all wealth (since past savings would purchase fewer goods than they could have purchased before the tax was enacted). In practice, the provisions of the tax might become very complicated and therefore difficult to administer and to obey. And the adoption by the federal government of a broad-based consumption tax would intrude on a tax area traditionally reserved for the states. Henderson is also concerned that the introduction of an easy source of revenue like the value-added tax would encourage more federal spending.

Henderson expects that future federal deficits will be reduced by a combination of policies, including some reduction in spending and some broadening of the income taxes. However, he also believes that spending cuts and income taxes may have to be supplemented by excise taxes and perhaps by a value-added tax or sales tax to produce the necessary revenues.

The graduated consumption tax

Henry Aaron and Harvey Galper believe that the income tax is flawed in fundamental respects and argue that no amount of tinkering will correct some of the defects. The measurement of real income during periods of inflation is extremely difficult, and there is even disagreement about how the necessary adjustments should be made and how far they should go. Under an income tax, capital gains should be taxed as they accrue, but this principle cannot be applied in practice. The averaging provisions of the income tax moderate the effect on tax liabilities of short-term fluctuations in income, but they do nothing to ameliorate the differences arising from variations in income over a lifetime. By taxing returns to saving, the income tax falls more heavily on future than on present consumption. Numerous special provisions have been adopted to cope with these problems, but they have created serious inequities among taxpayers in similar economic circumstances, introduced huge distortions in the economy, and increased the cost of compliance and administration.

The only remedy, Aaron and Galper argue, is to substitute for the income tax a tax on consumption plus gifts and bequests. Such a tax base is simply the familiar economic definition of accrued income with the time period extended from one year to a lifetime and expressed in present value terms. For this reason, they refer to their tax as a "lifetime income" tax. Aaron and Galper choose a rate schedule that replicates the present law's distribution of taxes by income classes.

The consumption tax does not tax saving and therefore does not encourage current against future consumption. Aaron and Galper regard this as a much fairer result than that achieved by an income tax. The problems of measuring capital income during an inflation would be avoided, and the decision to realize or not to realize capital income would be independent of the tax system.

Some economists prefer a consumption tax to an income tax because it would provide greater incentives to save and would probably increase saving. Aaron and Galper hold that this is only a secondary argument in favor of either a consumption tax or the lifetime income tax they propose. A reduction in the federal deficit, they argue, is a more effective and more direct way to achieve this end. For Aaron and Galper, the major purpose of the tax they advocate is to improve the fairness of the tax system and reduce inefficiency, with any increase in saving that might be generated only an incidental advantage.

In principle a consumption tax does not require a corporation income tax to accompany it, but Aaron and Galper believe that in practice it would be necessary to have a corporation tax. They propose a tax on the cash flow of corporations, which would be calculated by subtracting all business outlays, including investment, from total receipts, including borrowing. Such a tax would fall on cash payments to foreign persons and entities not subject to U.S. taxation. In addition, the expensing of investment gives the government a share in returns that differs from the government's borrowing rate. If a corporation earns more than that rate, the government shares in the excess to the extent of the cash flow tax rate; if the corporation earns less, the government would share in the loss to the same extent.

The authors concede that some new problems would arise under the tax base they propose. It would be necessary to keep track of all capital flows, not just those that are associated with the measurement of income. Special transition rules would be needed to avoid taxing people (like the aged) who consume out of previously taxed income. In fashioning rules, policymakers would have to choose between simple but arbitrary adjustments and those that are individually calculated but complex. Going to a corporate cash flow tax would also require transition rules to deal with existing capital and debt. Other rules would be needed to deal with U.S. income of foreign investors, foreign income of U.S. citizens, and assets of those who immigrate and emigrate.

Evaluation of options

The conference discussion began with an examination by a number of participants of the reasons why so many complications have been introduced into the Internal Revenue Code. Part of the problem is that there have been fundamental changes in the process of tax legislation. Twenty-five years ago, the tax writing committees were smaller, a few key persons made most of the decisions, and tax bills were marked up in executive sessions. Today, the number of persons involved in tax legislation in the executive branch and in Congress is much larger, and the influence of tax lobbyists has increased. Some of the participants felt that this influence can be curbed only by reforming congressional campaign financing. Others suggested that the tax committees should return to closed executive sessions when making legislative decisions.

It was also pointed out that in recent years Congress has been trying to do too much with the tax laws. Deductions or credits have been introduced to achieve such diverse objectives as conserving energy, creating jobs for disadvantaged groups, encouraging investment, and increasing foreign trade. Such provisions are not only inefficient and costly, but they also greatly complicate the Internal Revenue Code. The lack of simplicity contributes strongly to the decline in popularity of the income taxes. Most of the participants felt that it would be desirable to eliminate tax preferences and use the revenue to reduce tax rates. But they differed on whether such an approach is practical.

One group of participants argued that the piecemeal approach followed in the past will not get very far because of the resistance of the lobbyists against any inroads into the tax preferences of their clients. They felt it would be necessary to enlist the support of a broad constituency to mount a successful tax reform effort, and in general they supported base broadening along the lines of the Bradley-Gephardt bill and similar proposals. These proposals fall short of full, comprehensive income taxation for practical reasons, but this was regarded by some as their strength. They argued that political compromises will be necessary to simplify the income tax, and that it is better to make these compromises before the proposal is seriously considered rather than have it rejected out of hand.

Another view was that there is really no hope of broadening the income tax base sufficiently to provide the revenue needed for significant rate reduction. Moreover, Congress has already begun weeding out the worst of the tax preferences in the interest of generating more revenues to reduce the prospective deficits. Thus, according to this view, the income tax may be improved, but not to the extent envisaged by the supporters of comprehensive taxation.

It was generally agreed that the next big battle in tax policy will be to raise revenues in order to close the deficit. Those who believe that income tax reform will not raise enough revenue argued that a new revenue source will be needed. The source mentioned most frequently is the value-added tax, a tax which is now levied almost universally in Western Europe.

Opinion about the value-added tax was divided. Some felt that it should be rejected because it would put a heavy burden on low-income families. At best, the tax would be proportional to income and not progressive. Others warned that compliance and administration under the value-added tax is not as easy as its proponents believe. In practice, many countries have greatly complicated their value-added taxes by providing numerous exemptions or preferential rates for such items as food, shelter, and medicine. Proponents of the value-added tax were aware of these problems, but they nevertheless supported it as a last resort in the quest for additional revenue.

The most spirited discussion of the conference concerned the graduated consumption tax, which is still another alternative to the income tax. The opposition to the consumption tax came mainly from those who believe that saving should not be exempt from taxation for reasons of equity. They pointed out that consumption tax advocates concede the appeal of the income tax to the public by describing their tax as a type of income tax (for example, Aaron and Galper call theirs a lifetime income tax; others call it a consumed income tax; and still others simply call it an income tax).

Proponents of the consumption tax countered by arguing that it is a much fairer tax than the income tax precisely because it does not tax saving and therefore does not discriminate against future consumption. They felt that the income tax problems raised by Graetz will not be solved and that continuation of the present inequities and distortions would be intolerable.

The issue of fairness was not resolved, but it was generally agreed that the viability of the consumption tax depended on whether it could remain a fairly clean tax after going through the legislative process. Several speakers maintained that there is as little reason to expect Congress to enact a comprehensive consumption tax as there is to expect it to enact a comprehensive income tax. The same type of preferences that are now built into the income tax would doubtless reappear in the consumption tax, and the outcome would be a tax riddled with loopholes and exempting saving besides.

A major issue in the implementation of the consumption tax is the problem of untaxed accumulations of wealth. Aaron and Galper would tax gifts and bequests, with a lifetime exemption of $100,000. They argued that this approach would permit individuals to save for their retirement on a tax-free basis, yet it would discourage undue increases in the concentration of wealth due to gifts and bequests. They stressed that inclusion of gifts and bequests is essential to their proposal, because excluding them would leave a consumption tax base, which does not measure lifetime ability to pay.

Recent experience with the estate and gift taxes suggests that Congress is hardly likely to tax bequests and gifts greater than $100,000 in a lifetime when the gift and estate tax exemptions are scheduled to increase to $600,000 in 1987 under present law. Moreover, the present annual exclusion of $10,000 per year per recipient would allow large tax-free transfers unless it were reduced very substantially. A number of the participants were skeptical, therefore, about the possibility of enacting an effective tax on gifts and bequests in conjunction with a consumption tax and expressed concern that the distribution of wealth would become highly concentrated if the consumption tax were substituted for the income tax.

Although the conference did not resolve the issues, it did help to clarify the sources of the differences among views about tax reform. Moreover, opinion was unanimous that the proliferation of deductions, exclusions, and preferential tax rates has complicated the tax laws unnecessarily. Opinion was also unanimous that the impending federal deficits were much too large and that additional taxes as well as spending cuts will be needed to bring them down. Whether tax reform will produce significant revenues for this purpose will be decided by the nation's political process.

Lessons from Seven Decades
of Income Taxation

RICHARD GOODE

LAST OCTOBER a significant anniversary passed, little noticed and quite uncelebrated. Seventy years earlier, on October 3, 1913, President Woodrow Wilson approved the first income tax act under the Sixteenth Amendment. In the House of Representatives the leading advocates of the tax were Cordell Hull and John Nance Garner. The House Ways and Means Committee called the income tax "the fairest and cheapest of all taxes" and predicted that it would meet with general satisfaction and support.[1] Today even strong supporters of income taxation (of whom I am one) must acknowledge that there is widespread dissatisfaction with both the individual income tax and the corporation income tax.

Present discontents

Public opinion polls for the Advisory Commission on Intergovernmental Relations report that a plurality of adults regard the federal income tax as the worst (least fair) tax.[2] The pollsters do not tell us what people dislike about the tax, but a clue is given by the response to the question: what *one* change would do most to make the tax system more fair? About half of the respondents in May 1983, when offered a choice among six options (including "do not know"), chose "make the upper income taxpayers pay more." Opinions did not differ greatly among income classes, though making the rich pay more was least popular in the highest—and the lowest—income classes. The replies suggest that people are not so much dissatisfied with the progressive income tax ideal as with its imperfect application.

On the other hand, when asked which tax could best be used if the federal government had to raise a substantial amount of

1. H. Rept. 5, 63 Cong. 1 sess. (1913), reprinted in U.S. Bureau of Internal Revenue, *Internal Revenue Bulletin,* Cumulative Bulletin 1939-1, pt. 2 (January–June 1939), pp. 1–3.

2. Advisory Commission on Intergovernmental Relations, *Changing Public Attitudes on Governments and Taxes: A Commission Survey, 1983* (Washington, D.C.: ACIR, 1983), p. 13.

additional revenue, half of those questioned in 1983 chose a new national sales tax on all purchases other than food, and only one-fourth preferred increasing individual income taxes. (One-fourth did not know.) A sales tax, of course, is generally considered regressive even if food is exempt.

Critics have long stressed inequities in the form of differences in the income tax on similarly situated persons. These differences exist at each income level and are caused by unjustifiable exclusions and deductions. The provisions also reduce progressivity but appear not to eliminate it.

The justification of the corporation income tax has always been controversial. Some view it as not only an expedient revenue source but a contribution to progressivity and a means of tapping the ability to pay of large companies. Others concede that undistributed profits should be taxed to prevent tax-free accumulation on behalf of stockholders but argue that the application of both the corporate tax and the individual income tax to distributed profits results in unfair double taxation. During much of the history of income taxation in the United States, dividend recipients have benefited from some provision intended to mitigate the burden resulting from taxation at both the corporate and individual levels. At present, this takes the form of the exclusion of $100 of dividends from taxable income of individual stockholders ($200 for husbands and wives filing joint returns). More a gesture than a substantive concession, the small dividend exclusion may indicate that other issues have diverted attention from the basic question of how corporations should be taxed. The U.S. system differs from those of most other industrial countries. While all these countries tax corporate profits, only the Netherlands does as little as the United States to relieve shareholders of the corporate tax on distributed profits.

A frequent complaint is that the individual income tax is excessively complex. Unnecessary complexity confuses and alienates taxpayers and wastes scarce talents in socially unproductive activities of tax lawyers, accountants, and revenue agents. Many of the complaints on this score are ill informed. Complexity is rarely the product of careless or incompetent drafting of statutes, regulations, or forms, though some of the documents could benefit from sterner editing. In our complex economy, a satisfactory income tax cannot be simple. But the cause of much complexity is the special provisions that are excrescences rather than essential features of income taxation. The 1983 individual income tax return (form 1040), for example, includes no less than eight possible adjustments to income and seven tax credits—most of which must be supported by separate forms or schedules. These are in addition to the schedules for capital gains and losses, itemized deductions, and the alternative minimum tax.

Economists point to inefficiencies in resource use attributable to provisions of both the individual income tax and the corporate tax. Most of those who have studied the subject think that these inefficiencies have recently increased greatly. There are difficulties and hidden differences of opinion in defining efficiency to which I shall return later. Here I shall merely assert that the present income taxes induce many changes in business organization, investment, and production that were not accurately foreseen and that fail to contribute to productivity, growth, and stability. Examples include tax-induced mergers, highly leveraged real estate ventures organized as limited partnerships, and questionable projects financed by tax-exempt industrial development bonds. Less conspicuous are wide differences in effective tax rates on returns from investments in various kinds of capital equipment; these resulted from the combination of the investment credit and the adoption in 1981 of the Accelerated Cost Recovery System. The new cost recovery system abandoned the relationship between the write-off of capital costs and the useful life of equipment and structures, a relationship which is a basic feature of commercial accounting and which had been a part of the income tax since 1913. This change inevitably resulted in different tax rates on economic income from various assets, and there is no reason to suppose that these differences correspond to a coherent ranking of the social desirability of investment in the assets.

The attractions of tax-favored investments are enhanced when part of the associated costs can be deducted against fully taxable income. The investor's return then comprises saving of tax on the other income as well as receipts from the tax-favored investment. Transactions expressly designed to exploit such possibilities are known as tax shelters. Their tax-avoidance possibilities have attracted the attention of the Treasury Department, Congress, and the press and have provoked some corrective legislation. Their economic aspects, while not wholly neglected, have been less widely appreciated. The presumption of economic inefficiency is especially strong because tax-sheltered investments that would produce not merely low returns but losses in the absence of taxation can be advantageous solely because of the tax saving.

Tax arbitrage   Tax shelters are too diverse and complex to survey generally in this paper.[3] Instead, I wish to comment briefly on a particular kind of transaction called tax arbitrage. This is the process of borrowing to acquire or hold financial or real assets whose return is either tax exempt or subject to a low tax rate and deducting the interest payments from fully taxable income. Tax arbitrage is a feature of the most notorious tax shelters, but it also enters into transactions that would not ordinarily be thought of as tax shelters. Opportunities for tax arbitrage are extensive, and the use of some of them requires no great skill or expense.

As a simple example of tax arbitrage, consider the case of a person subject to the top income tax rate of 50 percent who simultaneously borrows at, say, 13 percent and invests in tax-exempt municipal bonds yielding 10 percent. The net interest cost is 6.5 percent, which is 3.5 percentage points lower than the tax-free yield of 10 percent. To be sure, a person who used the bonds as collateral for the loan would be subject to having the interest deduction disallowed. But if the investor has other assets to use as collateral and arranges matters carefully, the deduction will be allowable, even though the borrowing in fact made possible the acquisition of the tax-exempt bonds. Another example of tax arbitrage is to borrow to buy growth stocks or bonds selling at a deep discount. The interest on the loan can be deducted immediately against fully taxable income while capital gains are deferred or, if realized, are taxed at only 40 percent of the regular rate (provided the stock is held a year or more). A further example is to borrow and invest the proceeds in an individual retirement account, deferring tax for perhaps many years on the income that is building up in the account while immediately deducting the interest payment against taxable income.

Still other, less plain, examples of tax arbitrage are owning a principal residence or a vacation house subject to a mortgage or buying a car or other consumer durable with installment credit. The interest payments may be deducted against taxable income, but the rental value of the house, car, or other durable need not be reported as taxable income. Because money is fungible, it is not essential that borrowing be explicitly linked to the tax-preferred asset; any interest payment may be regarded as a cost of acquiring or holding tax-preferred assets equal in value to the

---

3. See *Proposals Relating to Tax Shelters and Other Tax-Motivated Transactions,* Joint Committee Print, prepared by the Joint Committee on Taxation, 98 Cong. 2 sess. (Government Printing Office, 1984).

debt. Like M. Jourdain, who spoke prose for more than forty years without knowing it, most middle-class families have engaged in tax arbitrage, even though they may not know it.

More complex and potentially more lucrative is tax arbitrage with investments in assets eligible for accelerated capital cost recovery and in many cases investment tax credits. For example, a high-income person can invest in real estate or farming through a leveraged, limited partnership which will generate deductions sufficient to eliminate any current tax on the receipts and to reduce the tax on other income. The effective tax on the venture is negative in the sense that the after-tax return is greater than it would be if there were no income tax. Negative tax rates can also be obtained by less exotic arrangements. For example, a corporation subject to the regular tax rate of 46 percent on income from previous investments can borrow to acquire a piece of equipment eligible for an investment tax credit of 10 percent and for capital cost recovery deductions at a more rapid rate than economic depreciation.

The cost recovery provisions of the Economic Recovery Tax Act of 1981 widened opportunities for tax arbitrage by liberalizing capital cost recovery deductions and restrictions on the use of individual retirement accounts. However, the reduction of the top rate of individual income tax from 70 percent to 50 percent reduced the gains possible for top-income persons. Deduction of interest paid by individuals to purchase investments is subject to a limit equal to the taxpayer's net investment income (other than capital gains) plus $10,000 (plus an additional $15,000 when the debt is incurred to acquire ownership of a family business); excess payments may be carried forward and deducted against investment income in future years.

A new source of discontent is the loss of revenue caused by the massive tax cuts of 1981. Originally estimated to rise from $38 billion in fiscal year 1982 to $286 billion in fiscal year 1987, the cuts were partly rescinded in 1982.[4] The tax reductions and rapidly growing defense expenditures are mainly responsible for the alarmingly large budget deficits now projected as far ahead as the forecasters can see. It has been asserted that the corporation income tax has been virtually eliminated. That is an exaggeration.

---

4. Joseph A. Pechman and Barry P. Bosworth, "The Budget and the Economy," in Joseph A. Pechman, ed., *Setting National Priorities: The 1983 Budget* (Brookings Institution, 1982), p. 29; Harvey Galper, "Tax Policy," in Joseph A. Pechman, ed., *Setting National Priorities: The 1984 Budget* (Brookings Institution, 1983), p. 176.

The tax has been sharply, but not uniformly, reduced. As explained earlier, effective tax rates on the returns from various assets differ widely.

How we got here

Complaints about the individual and corporation income taxes probably built up over the long period during which revenue from these taxes grew in relation to gross national product and other sources of federal revenue. The taxes on income and profits yielded about 12.5 percent of total federal receipts in the fiscal years 1914–16. Their share rose to almost 60 percent during World War I; after falling moderately in the 1920s and more sharply in the 1930s, it rose again to more than 60 percent during World War II and continued at that level or higher until recently. The upward trend in federal revenues meant that the share of income taxes in GNP increased more than their share in federal revenue. In the first few years, they absorbed only about one-quarter of 1 percent of GNP; this figure reached about 3 percent during World War I; in the 1970s, it was about 11 percent.[5] Until World War II, the corporate tax yielded more than the individual income tax; during the war the individual tax somewhat surpassed the corporate income and excess profits taxes; after the war the corporate share fell—to less than one-half that of the individual income tax in the 1960s and to about one-third in the 1970s.[6]

Only recently did the unfavorable view of the income tax become the opinion of a plurality of citizens. A poll taken in 1972 found that respondents considered the federal income tax the fairest of all the major taxes used by the federal, state, and local governments. There were, however, signs of polarization, for a sizable minority considered the federal income tax the least fair.[7]

A likely cause of the abrupt decline in the public opinion rating of the individual income tax after 1972 was its interaction with inflation. Over the years 1972–83, the consumer price index rose by 138 percent, more than it had increased from the end of World War II up to 1972. With personal exemptions and nominal rates in the federal income tax unchanged in 1972–78, the decline in the real value of the exemptions and bracket creep caused the

5. GNP statistics from U.S. Census Bureau, *Historical Statistics of the United States: Colonial Times to 1970*, pt. 1, p. 224; *Economic Report of the President, February 1983*, p. 163.

6. For revenue statistics, see Richard Goode, *The Individual Income Tax*, rev. ed. (Brookings Institution, 1976), pp. 301–02; *Economic Report of the President, February 1983*, table B-72.

7. Advisory Commission on Intergovernmental Relations, *Changing Public Attitudes*, pp. 39, 42.

taxes of many persons to increase faster than their real income. Increases in personal exemptions and the zero bracket amount effective in 1979 failed to check this movement. Individual income tax liabilities increased, with some interruptions, from 9.8 percent of total personal income in 1972 to 11.7 percent in 1981.[8]

For corporations, inflation reduced the real value of depreciation allowances for tax purposes, which were based on historical cost. Offsetting changes were liberalization of depreciation methods by shortening useful lives and reduction of the corporate tax rate from 48 percent to 46 percent, effective in 1979. Over the period 1972–81, the effective rate of federal corporate income tax declined when measured against profits calculated with standardized, historical-cost depreciation methods.[9] However, there was no clear trend in that period in effective rates of total (federal and state) corporate taxes measured in relation to profits adjusted for the increased cost of capital consumption and for inventory valuation gains.[10]

Tax preferences

Another factor that may have contributed to the declining prestige of the income tax is the growth of tax preferences that many people consider unjustified and the existence of preferences that benefit mainly the rich. These are now publicized and quantified under the name "tax expenditures" in a special budget analysis and in congressional reports. Despite some reservations about the concept and some differences of opinion about the items to be included, I shall use the tax expenditure statistics because they are widely disseminated and convenient.

There was a rapid increase in the number of tax expenditures and in their revenue cost, especially after 1979. The Joint Committee on Taxation and the Congressional Budget Office identified 104 tax expenditures in effect in fiscal year 1982. Between 1971 and 1982, tax expenditures grew from the equivalent of 25 percent of federal revenue (4.6 percent of GNP) to 41 percent of federal revenue and about 8.4 percent of GNP. The biggest ones, however, are of long standing. About 35 percent of the estimated fiscal year 1982 tax expenditures related to items that had never been subject to income tax (including social security benefits); 63 percent to provisions predating World War II; 83 percent to provisions in

---

8. Joseph A. Pechman, *Federal Tax Policy*, 4th ed. (Brookings Institution, 1983), p. 332.

9. Ibid., pp. 144, 364–65.

10. Derived from *Economic Report of the President, February 1983*, p. 257.

effect by 1950; and 95 percent to provisions introduced by 1970.[11] The increase in tax expenditures is due mainly to greater use of old provisions. Nevertheless, the proliferation of tax expenditures is disturbing and may become more costly as people learn how to exploit them more fully.

Provisions now classified as tax expenditures came about in different ways. By no means all of them were intended to subsidize favored activities or to relieve hardship.[12] The deduction of all interest payments, including interest on home mortgages and consumer credit, has been in the law since 1913. It seems to have been adopted to avoid a difficult distinction between interest payments that are costs of earning taxable income and other payments. The deduction for nonbusiness taxes, which also dates from 1913, may have been motivated by a desire to avoid double taxation in the literal sense. It was not designed to help state and local governments, since federal taxes (including the income tax itself) as well as state and local taxes were originally deductible. In retrospect, the deductions for mortgage interest and property taxes have been rationalized as incentives for home ownership.

The exclusion from federally taxed income of interest on state and local securities, another feature of the 1913 act, responded to a generally accepted constitutional doctrine of the time. The exclusion from employees' taxable income of pension contributions by employers (adopted in 1921) and of employer contributions for medical insurance (permitted by an Internal Revenue Service ruling in 1943 and codified in 1954) probably reflected the prevailing reluctance to tax unrealized or imputed income.

Individual retirement plans, allowed on a limited scale in 1974 and greatly broadened later, were initially intended to lessen discrimination by extending the preferential treatment of employer plans rather than restricting it. The exclusion of social security benefits from taxable income was introduced by administrative ruling in 1941 shortly after monthly benefits were first paid, apparently with little or no consideration of its future significance.

The introduction in 1917 of the deduction for charitable contributions may have been the first important example of a deliberate incentive or subsidy provision. It was supported as a means of

---

11. Congressional Budget Office, *Tax Expenditures: Budget Control Options and Five-Year Projections for Fiscal Years 1983–1987* (GPO, 1982), p. 12 and tables C-1 and C-2.

12. See Goode, *The Individual Income Tax,* chap. 6, "Exclusions from Taxable Income," and chap. 7, "Personal Deductions"; C. Harry Kahn, *Personal Deductions in the Federal Income Tax* (Princeton University Press for the National Bureau of Economic Research, 1960).

preventing the increased taxes required for war finance from crowding out gifts for worthy causes. Incentive considerations appear to have been decisive in the introduction of a preferential rate for capital gains in 1921, although this occurred at a time when regular rates were being sharply reduced. Other incentive provisions include accelerated depreciation, the investment tax credit, percentage depletion, and several less significant items.

Specifically intended to relieve hardship, the medical expense deduction was originally adopted in 1942 at a time of high wartime tax rates. Arguably in the same category are the exclusion of veterans' benefits and workers' compensation (dating from 1917 and 1918, respectively) and the extra exemption for the elderly (adopted in 1948).

Popular dissatisfaction with the present state of the income tax may also be associated with beliefs about the prevalence of abuses in the form of excessive deductions for business expenses (the symbolic three-martini lunch); evasion (the underground economy); and the use of improper tax shelters by public figures, including some high government officials. The successful lobbying campaign by banks and other financial institutions for repeal of withholding of tax on interest and dividends may have strengthened cynicism. The extent of abuses is likely exaggerated in the public mind, but that guess cannot be confirmed in the absence of hard evidence on either the popular beliefs or the facts.

The latest estimates of tax evasion published by the Internal Revenue Service are disturbing. They place the 1981 loss of revenue from legally earned income at $68.5 billion for individuals and $6.2 billion for corporations. I calculate this as equivalent to 23 percent of individuals' reported liabilities before credits and about 6 percent for corporations. (These figures reflect nonfiling, underreporting of income, and overstatement of deductions but for individuals do not include failure to pay reported liabilities.) In addition, the Internal Revenue Service estimates tax evasion of $9 billion on illegal income from drug traffic, illegal gambling, and prostitution.[13] The IRS calculations should be viewed cautiously. Some experts think the figures for underreporting of legal income and the associated tax gap are too high. Furthermore, the estimates of tax evasion on illegal income are especially tenuous for statistical reasons, and because illegal income usually dries up when discovered and taxed.

13. Internal Revenue Service, *Income Tax Compliance Research: Estimates for 1973–1981* (GPO, 1983), p. 3.

The shortcomings of the income tax have been extensively publicized in recent years by journalists and politicians. Candidate Jimmy Carter called the tax "a disgrace to the human race." Experts who favored the income tax provided much of the material for the journalists and politicians by exposing gaps between the ideal and the actual tax in detailed and perhaps excessively critical writings.

The more conservative climate of opinion that led to the nomination and election of Jimmy Carter and Ronald Reagan encouraged Americans to believe that they were overtaxed, though the ratio of taxation to GNP was lower in the United States than in all other industrial countries except Japan and in some years Switzerland.[14] Many people were receptive to supply-side arguments and were bored by—or antagonistic to—calls for income redistribution through progressive taxation and welfare expenditures. If the politics of Woodrow Wilson's New Freedom had favored the introduction of the income tax in 1913, the balance of political forces of 1973 and of 1983 allowed the tax to be eroded but not eliminated.

Proposed reforms

Last and perhaps not least among the factors damaging the prestige of the income tax is the attraction of many economists to the consumption tax base, which they consider fairer and economically preferable to income taxation. The doctrine is not new; in the mid-nineteenth century John Stuart Mill subscribed to it. But a direct tax on consumption (known as an expenditure tax) was long considered impractical, and it has gained numerous adherents only in the past ten to fifteen years.

Despite widespread dissatisfaction with the present state of the income taxes, there is now no consensus in favor of either their reinvigoration or their replacement. A perennial proposal for reform of the individual income tax is the introduction of a comprehensive tax with lower, graduated rates, to be achieved by eliminating exclusions from the tax base and deductions not required for the accurate measurement of economic income. The parallel proposal for corporations is to rehabilitate the corporation income tax by bringing the definition of taxable profits as close to the economic concept as feasible; this would require the replacement of the accelerated cost recovery system by depreciation allowances related to the loss of useful life as well as the indexing

14. Organization for Economic Cooperation and Development, *Revenue Statistics of OECD Member Countries 1965–1982* (Paris: OECD, 1983), p. 68.

for inflation of depreciation allowances and interest payments and receipts. The tax rate would be reduced; tax relief might or might not be allowed for dividends.

Proposals that depart from income tax traditions include the replacement of the individual income tax by a flat-rate tax on all income, but with personal exemptions, or by a graduated expenditure tax or a sales tax. For corporations, the present tax might be replaced by a cash flow tax that would apply to the excess of receipts from sales of goods and services over purchases, without deduction of interest or dividend payments.

I have set out the proposals for change in more or less pure form. Modifications, compromises, and partial versions are possible. And terminology is unstandardized. Those who are attracted to the comprehensive income tax idea may attach it to proposals for limited base broadening. Recently "flat tax" has come to be considered an appealing term and has been applied to proposals that provide for graduated rates and appreciable progressivity.

My reading of the lessons

To draw lessons from our experience with the individual and corporate income taxes is to exercise judgment with large subjective elements. My reading classifies a long list of lessons under four headings: popular and congressional attitudes; the work of tax specialists; operating experience; and reform strategy and tactics. Others may identify different lessons.

Popular and Congressional Attitudes

1. There is strong support for progressive taxation but skepticism about the extent to which it is, or will be, applied. The evidence of support is not only the recent public opinion polls but frequent endorsements of ability to pay and the inclusion of graduated rates in all individual income tax acts since 1913. Progressive income tax rates are in effect in all other industrial countries, and it is unlikely that Americans have a radically different attitude toward this basic issue. I infer that a true flat-rate income tax would be unacceptable to the majority.

2. Although public discussion of ability to pay and progressivity runs in terms of an income base, it is doubtful whether the general public or members of Congress clearly understand the differences between the income and consumption bases and have a settled preference. I can well imagine that stories about miserly millionaires who would pay little under an expenditure tax would attract attention and indignation, but perhaps no more than similar stories about millionaires who escape the income tax. I find little evidence

of wide concern about wealth inequality and suspect that the majority would not be greatly impressed by the argument that a consumption tax would remove a desirable check on wealth accumulation.

3. Responses to the opinion poll conducted by the Advisory Commission on Intergovernmental Relations seem inconsistent. Perhaps they can be reconciled by inferring that, while the people's ideal is a progressive tax, they are so skeptical about its effective application that they believe a sales tax would collect more from the rich than would an increase in the present income tax. In the late Middle Ages and early modern period, many writers advocated indirect taxes as a means of hitting the privileged members of the clergy and nobility, who escaped existing direct taxes. Possibly, the simplicity and partly concealed (or obscured) burden of the sales tax are factors in its current appeal.

4. The interaction between the income taxes and inflation has been poorly apprehended, and asymmetric attitudes have formed to the detriment of tax policy. As I earlier suggested, bracket creep probably was a major cause of the declining reputation of the income tax in the 1970s. Congress responded by indexing the brackets and personal exemptions, beginning in 1985—a provision that may soon be eliminated in the search for revenue. The liberalization of capital cost recovery provisions for taxing profits was supported partly as a means of compensating for the erosion of the real value of historical cost depreciation allowances. There has been some recognition of the adverse effects on recipients of interest income, although no explicit relief has been extended to them. The tax advantages enjoyed by debtors have been disregarded. Inflation forced up nominal interest rates to compensate lenders for the falling real value of loans, though with a lag and imperfectly. The compensation for inflation received by lenders and paid by borrowers is not interest in the real sense but amortization of the debt. The income tax laws failed to recognize this. Hence, lenders were overtaxed, often suffering negative real after-tax returns. Borrowers, on the other hand, were undertaxed because they were allowed to deduct not only real interest but partial amortization of debt. Lending was discouraged and borrowing encouraged. If, as I fear it is realistic to expect, inflation continues to be a chronic disease, it will be highly important to try to deal with both sides of the tax distortion, difficult as that would be.

5. The tendency of tax specialists to equate neutrality with equity and economic efficiency is neither understood nor accepted

by the general public and politicians. As regards equity, departures from neutrality are considered unfair when they appear to serve no agreed, socially useful purpose but are usually acceptable if they do serve such a purpose. As for efficiency, I find no general agreement on a clear standard. Many economists tend to take the patterns of prices, production, and consumption set in free markets as the standard and to classify departures from them as inefficient per se. This approach has appeal if—and only if—one believes that real-world markets correspond reasonably well to the theoretical conditions of perfect information, rationality, competition, mobility . . . in short, if one believes that the markets are efficient. Critics may detect circular reasoning here. Another approach, which I think is acceptable in principle to most legislators, though often carelessly followed or ignored, is that a judgment about efficiency must compare benefits and costs, even if roughly or intuitively. A tax provision is efficient if it furthers an agreed objective at reasonable direct and indirect costs (somehow appraised). To illustrate, members of Congress are unlikely to be impressed by an economist's assertion that the investment tax credit is inefficient because it encourages investment in equipment relative to structures. Presumably, that is what Congress intended when it allowed the credit for equipment but not for structures. But a scrupulous legislator would be interested in an examination of the probable impact on the amount of investment, the consequences for broader economic objectives, and the revenue costs.

6. Although simplification is universally endorsed, interest groups and Congress have been unwilling to pay much for it in terms of their primary objectives and indeed have readily accepted complications to attain their purposes. An exception to this may have been the evolution from capital cost recovery provisions based on elaborate tables of useful lives, which in turn were drawn from economic and engineering studies, to the accelerated cost recovery provisions based on four classes of assets with uniform rates; in my opinion, however, the primary objective was more rapid write-offs, with simplification a minor side benefit.

7. Some so-called tax expenditures are associated with deeply embedded beliefs about fairness and public policy. Examples include the preferential treatment of owner-occupied houses, the medical expense deduction, and the deduction for charitable contributions. It seems likely that the preferential treatment of these and some other esteemed items will survive efforts to broaden the income tax base and that it would continue under an expenditure tax.

8. For most people, corporations are real entities, not legal fictions or veils. It follows that the majority think that corporations should pay their "fair" share of taxes, though that is not precisely defined. Many limited partnerships resemble corporations in essential respects and, if better understood, no doubt would also be regarded as proper taxable entities. Popular attitudes do not necessarily oppose some alleviation of the tax burden on dividends or other distributions.

The Work of Tax Specialists

9. My comments on the lessons to be drawn about the work of tax specialists no doubt are especially subjective. Many economists and lawyers have taken a perfectionist attitude toward income taxation while neglecting the shortcomings of other taxes that are now in use or that might be adopted. It seems to me that claims about the defects of the existing individual and corporate income taxes and the gains from reforms have often been exaggerated. I refer to both the simplistic assertions of supply-siders and the arcane calculations of econometricians. What the supply-siders say is easy to understand but hard to believe. What the econometricians write is hard to understand but easy to misinterpret.

Not content with useful, if uncertain, estimates of effects on revenue, hours worked, and amounts saved, econometricians now produce numerical estimates of the influence of taxation on aggregate economic welfare.[15] They often shock readers (mercifully including few journalists and legislators) by estimates of seemingly huge losses or gains. They skate boldly over the thin ice covering deep questions: Can the feelings of millions of individuals be objectively measured and meaningfully summed? Are people's preferences so consistent and stable that they can be projected ahead for fifty to one hundred years, as implied by some models? Can economic welfare be separated from general welfare? From justice in distribution? Are the estimates purely technical descriptions, as some writers aver, or are they examples of moral arithmetic, unavoidably normative, as the word welfare connotes in common usage? As an old-fashioned economist and a citizen, I may say that at this stage quantitative estimates of welfare gains and losses due to tax provisions strike me as unhelpful for policy

---

15. See, for example, Arnold C. Harberger, *Taxation and Welfare* (Little, Brown, 1974); John B. Shoven, "Applied General-Equilibrium Tax Modeling," *International Monetary Fund Staff Papers,* vol. 30 (June 1983), pp. 394–420.

appraisal. I should add that refinement of estimates of the objective effects of taxes seems to me a practical and useful endeavor.

10. Both the econometric studies just mentioned and many of the less ambitious analyses that economists have long undertaken are based on simplified models of the economy and of behavior that seem highly unrealistic. Frequently it is assumed that producers and consumers are fully informed of all costs and prices, that producers maximize profits, that everyone can lend or borrow at known risk-adjusted rates of interest, and that people rationally equate present and future income and outgo over their lifetime by discounting at an appropriate rate. Despite recurring recessions, many analyses and policy prescriptions are based on the assumption that labor and capital are always fully employed. And in the absence of observed values, hypothetical parameters are often relied upon. Given the complexity of the real world, simplification is unavoidable, but assumptions should be exposed, the sensitivity of results to both estimated and hypothetical values should be examined, and modesty about conclusions and policy prescriptions should be observed.

11. Tax specialists have often failed to explain clearly to opinion leaders their research and recommendations. This is only partly due to the complexity of the subject matter. Academic prestige attaches mainly to writings addressed to other specialists, and contemporary taste in the economics profession favors formal presentation, preferably with a good deal of mathematics. Not only papers dealing with recondite theoretical points, but treatments of mundane questions of policy and administration, are frequently inaccessible to policymakers and their advisers. By default, charlatans or special pleaders too often dominate public discussion.

12. The practical difficulties of applying new income tax provisions have sometimes been underestimated. Probably this is true to an even greater degree for wholly new taxes such as a direct tax on consumption expenditures. The fact is that only two countries—India and Sri Lanka—have tried that tax, and in both it was a dismal failure. Granted that conditions in the United States differ greatly from those in India and Sri Lanka, I think that an expenditure tax would be more difficult to apply fairly than the income tax, not easier as its advocates now assert.[16]

16. Goode, *The Individual Income Tax,* pp. 29–31. See also Richard E. Slitor, "Administrative Aspects of Expenditures Taxation," in Richard A. Musgrave, ed., *Broad-Based Taxes: New Options and Sources* (Johns Hopkins University Press, 1973), pp. 227–63; Michael J. Graetz, "Expenditure Tax Design," in Joseph A. Pechman, ed., *What Should Be Taxed? Income or Expenditure?* (Brookings Institution, 1980), pp. 161–276.

Operating Experience

13. Tax arbitrage has become a potent threat to equity, revenue, and rational economic policy. Short of comprehensive reforms, further limitations on the interest deduction could help check arbitrage. For individuals, the present limitation on the deduction of investment interest could be tightened. For corporations, the issue is more controversial and technically more difficult. Two approaches that may merit study are (1) a requirement that corporations allocate interest deductions proportionately between taxable and nontaxable income and (2) reinstatement of a rule included in the early income tax acts that limited a corporation's interest deduction to an amount attributable to indebtedness not exceeding a stated multiple of its equity capital.[17] Limitations on the interest deduction would be reinforced if accompanied by fuller taxation of capital gains.

14. Little preferences (tax expenditures) grow into big ones as conditions change and as tax advisers, their clients, and the broad public learn to exploit them. A prominent example is the exclusion from taxable income of social security retirement and disability benefits. Of negligible significance when established by administrative ruling, the revenue cost had grown to $2.4 billion by 1970 and to $17.4 billion by 1983. The exclusion from employees' income of premiums for medical insurance and medical benefits provided by employers was estimated to cost $1.4 billion in 1970 and had increased to $18.6 billion by 1983.[18] In 1970, it appeared that all but a small amount of tax-exempt state and local bonds were for general government purposes. Recently, there has been a rapid growth in the use of tax-exempt bonds for industrial development, pollution control, owner-occupied housing, and rental housing. Many of the projects financed by industrial revenue bonds fail to qualify as innovative ventures likely to improve productivity and the country's international competitive position; according to a recent report, three of the four largest beneficiaries

17. The 1909 act, which imposed a tax on corporate profits before the Sixteenth Amendment became effective, allowed a corporation to deduct interest only on an amount of indebtedness not exceeding its capital stock. The rule was liberalized in 1913 and was dropped after a few years. See Roy G. Blakey and Gladys C. Blakey, *The Federal Income Tax* (Longmans, Green, 1940), pp. 97, 167–68; Edwin R. A. Seligman, *The Income Tax: A Study of the History, Theory, and Practice of Income Taxation at Home and Abroad,* 2d ed. (Macmillan, 1921), p. 685.

18. *General Tax Reform,* Panel Discussions before the House Committee on Ways and Means, 93 Cong. 1 sess. (GPO, 1973), pt. 1, pp. 29–30; Goode, *The Individual Income Tax,* p. 310; Congressional Budget Office, *Tax Expenditures: Current Issues and Five-Year Budget Projections for Fiscal Years 1984–1988* (GPO, 1983), p. 18.

since 1977 are K Mart Corporation, Kroger Company, and McDonald's Corporation.[19] The nontraditional uses of bonds cost the federal government an estimated $6.6 billion in revenue loss in 1983, compared with a loss of $10.4 billion for bonds for general state and local government purposes.[20] The lesson, if it needs pointing up, is that all proposals for new tax preferences, however small and innocuous they may appear, should be severely scrutinized.

15. When inequities attract attention, there has been a tendency to compensate by extending benefits rather than restricting them. Examples are individual retirement accounts and capital gains treatment for income from coal and iron ore royalties, patent royalties, timber cutting, livestock, and sale of unharvested crops. This has contributed to the weakness of the income tax and the loss of esteem for it.

16. Some reforms enacted in haste have been repealed at leisure. An example is a provision requiring persons receiving property by bequest to carry over the previous owner's basis when computing capital gains. Originally scheduled to take effect in 1977, it was intended to close a big loophole—the complete escape from taxation of capital gains that the decedent had not realized during life. Complaints about alleged compliance difficulties led first to postponement of the provision and then to its repeal before it was applied. Another example is withholding of tax on dividends and interest, enacted in 1982 to check widespread evasion but repealed in 1983 before it became effective (except for a residual requirement of withholding on payments to persons who have not supplied their taxpayer identification number or who have been identified as grossly underreporting receipts of dividends and interest). Incidentally, the 1913 act provided for withholding from dividends and interest as well as salaries and wages and rent, but because of unforeseen difficulties and hostile agitation, the provision was eliminated (except for nonresidents) by the 1917 act.[21] The lessons seem to be that difficulties and the strength of opposing interest groups should be carefully assessed in advance and that reformers should remain vigilant after apparent successes.

17. Enforcement has been inadequate. Audit coverage of individual income tax returns has fallen from 2.6 percent of all returns in 1976 to 1.3 percent in 1984. According to IRS estimates,

19. Robert J. Samuelson, "Tax-Exempt Bonds: A Study in Politics," *Washington Post,* February 22, 1984.

20. See sources listed in footnote 18.

21. Blakey and Blakey, *The Federal Income Tax,* pp. 79–80, 98, 101, 105, 143–55.

additional audits would return revenue equal to nine to ten times their cost.[22] To be sure, an allowance should be made for the costs and inconvenience that additional enforcement activities would impose on taxpayers; but, equally, better tax enforcement yields not only immediate revenue but improved voluntary compliance and respect for tax laws. I believe that the public would applaud efforts to combat evasion, if properly explained and publicized. Conversely, the experience of several countries with taxpayer amnesties—a measure recently proposed for the United States—suggests that an amnesty is an act of desperation that weakens confidence, encourages more evasion, and is unlikely to contribute much revenue even in the short run.

Reform Strategy and Tactics

18. Tax reform is very difficult but not impossible. The biggest reform of all was the introduction of the income tax itself in 1913, which had to overcome determined opposition and to await a constitutional amendment. Perhaps the most important examples of subsequent improvements include withholding on salaries and wages, adopted in 1943, which made feasible the conversion of the individual income tax to a mass tax covering most income recipients; current payment of estimated tax by both individuals and corporations, which was recognized as a logical extension of withholding; and income splitting between husbands and wives, adopted in 1948 to eliminate the advantages previously enjoyed by residents of community-property states. Significant but less far-reaching reforms include: limitation of the deduction of capital losses against other income (since 1924), with generous carryover of losses against gains (since 1942); curtailment of percentage depletion; curtailment of the deduction for indirect taxes; curtailment of the casualty loss deduction; curtailment of the medical expense deduction; a (generous) limit on the interest deduction for nonbusiness purposes; and the taxation of part of unemployment compensation and social security benefits. Some would include in the list the alternative minimum tax. In addition to these provisions that increased taxes, mention can be made of changes that reduced taxes. Examples: the standard deduction or zero-rate bracket (though its classification as an improvement may be questioned by some); averaging; the deduction for married couples when both work; the child-care credit.

22. Congressional Budget Office, *Reducing the Deficit: Spending and Revenue Options—Part III* (GPO, 1984), p. 211.

19. I find no clear connection between reforms and increases or decreases in tax rates. In the past, some tax specialists argued that reform was feasible only when taxes were being reduced, on the grounds that those adversely affected would resist being deprived of part of the reduction less strenuously than they would oppose an absolute increase in their taxes. Several reforms, however, have been made when taxes were going up, and the congressional budget process focuses attention on tax expenditures along with outright expenditures and changes in tax rates. Concern over excessive budget deficits may offer an opportunity to curtail or eliminate vulnerable tax preferences. The enactment of the perhaps extravagantly named Tax Equity and Fiscal Responsibility Act of 1982, as the result of a congressional initiative, is an important example. That act cut back some business benefits granted the previous year (by the seductively titled Economic Recovery Tax Act of 1981) and also some older tax preferences.

20. Popular and congressional attitudes on taxation usually (though not always) change slowly, but they do change. Reformers need persistence. Examples—good and bad—of persistence rewarded include the adoption of the Sixteenth Amendment and the income tax in 1913; legislative action on some supply-side proposals in recent years; and growing acceptance by academics of the consumption tax idea.

21. It is hard to win agreement on an income tax package that includes base broadening and lower nominal tax rates because of fears that nominal rates would rise in the future, thus fleecing the unsheltered taxpayers. This attitude is similar to the suspicion of both liberals and conservatives that a sales tax introduced at a low rate would prove to be such a big revenue producer that reliance on it would quickly increase. Reassurances can be given, but they will be unconvincing, because no administration and no Congress can commit its successors. We can only counsel confidence in the democratic process.

22. On the whole, I think experience favors an incrementalist approach to changes of policy and administration in taxation as in other areas. A series of small changes could improve the system greatly, provided most of them moved in the right direction. But something can be said for attacking deficiencies of the individual and corporate income taxes on a broad front in the hope of firing the imagination of supporters and dividing the opposition. Incrementalists need to have distant goals in mind while flexibly concentrating on near-term objectives.

23. In our system, executive leadership combined with proper respect for congressional opinion offers the best hope for major tax reforms. Congressional leaders may initiate and successfully push through some measures. But given the obstacles to reform, cooperation of the two branches is essential for great progress.

Tax Reform and the Tax Legislative Process

SLADE GORTON

IT MAY WELL BE that, just as those who enjoy sausage are best advised to stay away from watching its manufacture, those who are interested in tax policy are best advised not to observe the tax legislative process in the House of Representatives and Senate of the United States. With that proviso I should like to start with an incident that took place during the Senate debate over tax policy in April 1983. The Senate was scheduled to recess shortly after 5:00 A.M., just in time for the Easter recess. The Republican leadership, faced with senators' right of unlimited debate and unlimited amendments, decided that we would continue in session until the process had been completed. At about 11:00 P.M. on Thursday, Senate Majority leader Howard H. Baker, Jr., asked that every member who might propose an amendment reserve the right to do so, after which time unanimous consent would be sought to cut off further discussion.

Legislative marathons

The number of proposals rapidly rose from 20 to 30 to 40 to 50 and eventually began to run out of speed at number 62 or 63. At this point Senate Finance Committee leader Robert Dole, managing the bill, pointed out not quite sotto voce that there were plenty of lobbyists remaining in the gallery and if any of them would like to drop amendments over the railing they would be added to the unanimous consent agreement.

After a debate of about two hours or so on the first controversial amendment, a roll-call vote was begun at about 1:30 A.M. and generated an unhappy confrontation between one of the senators and the leadership. There are two cloakrooms immediately off the floor—one for Republicans and one for Democrats—for senators to read newspapers, rest, or engage in conversation. In each of those cloakrooms is a desk behind which a number of young staffers sit. Their primary duty is to know the location of every member at all times, particularly during night sessions when

33

some might be napping, so that they can get them to report for roll calls.

The Republican cloakroom staffers fell down on their duty for at least one Republican senator, who shall remain nameless. That senator missed the 1:30 A.M. roll call by a two- or three-minute margin. He was incensed at having this blight on his record, went to the floor leadership, and complained about the fact that he hadn't been found. He was told, "Well, I'm sorry senator, but George in the cloakroom couldn't find you." At this point, the senator left the floor, steamed into the cloakroom and found the two remaining staffers, George and Ann. Up to the desk he came and said, "Which one of you two is George?"

Under the circumstances, it may have been well that he did miss that vote. But many other members may not have been much more alert than he during the course of that evening's votes on a number of those amendments.

That debate, however, was important. In fact, it may have been pivotal in developing what had been a growing consensus for substantial budget deficit reductions beginning in the middle of last year into an agreement on a specific set of proposals that will at least provide a decent down payment on deficit reduction. The bill will include deficit reductions of $100 billion to $150 billion over the next three years.

Partisan disagreement over the need for deficit reduction ended at least two years ago. The problem for most of that two-year period has been that, while Republicans and conservatives generally were very much in favor of drastically lowering budget deficits, they wished to do it by taking social programs away from Democrats. Democrats, on the other hand, vied with Republicans in their denunciations of budget deficits, but by and large they wished to do so by taxing Republicans. With an administration and a Congress that is split in its control between the two parties, this effort was bound to fail.

Beginning only at about the 1983 Christmas recess, in my observation, did we reach a point where a significant number of members, Republicans and Democrats, conservatives and liberals, began to say that we were going to have to work on both the revenue and expenditure sides of the budget. Acceptance has grown not only for cutting the president's proposals for the defense budget but also for reducing the growth rate of social programs and for increasing the tax base.

It's the latter subject for which this conference has been convened. It's important for you constantly to keep in mind that the only reason we are likely to be successful at accomplishing any tax changes this year is that the down-payment package will contain cuts in both domestic and defense spending as well as revisions in the tax code. Even at the risk of $200 billion annual budget deficits or more, I think it unlikely that a tax increase standing alone would pass the Congress, much less be signed by the president of the United States. I am also convinced that the same thing will be true next year.

In any event, in the Senate and in the House as well, attention has gone first to the tax aspects of the down-payment proposal. The Senate at 5:00 A.M. on the Friday morning before the last recess did in fact approve a tax bill of about $50 billion over the course of the next three years. The House of Representatives approved a similar bill a few weeks earlier.

Lessons

There are some significant lessons to be learned from the passage of these slightly different tax bills. The first is that, although there are numerous modifications of the tax law in these bills, they do not contain an across-the-board and thorough tax reform. The best evidence of this is that the bills are more than 1,000 pages long and have not, I can assure you, been read from cover to cover by any member of the United States Senate or House of Representatives. This illustrates the weakness of the forces in favor of tax reform in a specific sense, as opposed to the general desire for drastic and fundamental changes in the tax system.

The second significant element in both the House and Senate versions of the tax bill is that there is no real change in the rate structure in these particular bills. The bills include some loophole closings, but in raw numbers more loopholes or preferences are created by these bills, at least the Senate version, than are closed.

What I have been describing is a process that will inevitably take place in the normal, if not every single, legislative cycle relating to taxation. Even though tax simplification and tax reform are easy and vital subjects for members to endorse, the fact is that in a society as complex as ours, there is an irresistible demand for tinkering with the system. I defer to no member of the United States Senate in the desire for a simpler, fairer, and a more understandable system. But during the progress of the tax bill through the Senate, I participated in at least half a dozen changes in committee and on the floor in favor of particular constituency groups in the state of Washington, which I represent. That is simply the way in which policies are determined by a group of elected officials in a free society.

So this leaves us with the question, assuming passage of a down payment in 1984, what is going to happen in 1985? It is clear to me, perhaps even clearer to members who have served in the Senate and the House considerably longer than I have, that there is more interest today in tax reform, at least in the abstract, than there has been in the past. Today there is more criticism of the income tax code on the basis of its perceived unfairness and ineffectiveness than there has been at any time in the last decade or perhaps since the establishment of the federal income tax early in this century.

There is at the same time more concern about budget deficits and more demands on the part of the public that we do something much more decisive than we are likely to accomplish next year about those deficits. People fear or criticize deficits because of the bad effects that they are almost universally judged to have on our present economic recovery—on employment, inflation, economic growth, interest rates, and the value of the dollar.

The president has announced that he has asked the secretary of the treasury to come up with meaningful and fundamental tax reform proposals conveniently to be published immediately after the presidential election is over. Democratic candidates are also unlikely before the election to do more than sketch with the broadest possible strokes the fundamental tax reforms that they support.

It also seems clear to me that when we take the second step in deficit reductions, spending and especially entitlement programs will be a major focus of attention. But we will in addition be faced with the proposition that the amount of the deficit reduction over the next three or four years that comes from a broader or more comprehensive base should be at least as great as that which comes from reductions in spending on social and defense programs.

Types of reform

Tax reform proposals fall into four basic categories, although those categories overlap. The first is the idea that there should be instituted a value-added tax or national sales tax, either alone or in combination with other tax reforms. This category basically entails a shift to a broad-based form of excise taxation. That idea has been around for some time. It suffered a serious, though not fatal, setback when Congressman Al Ullman of Oregon was defeated after talking about it in 1980. But the idea of adopting such a tax, a tax which is relatively widespread in most other industrialized democracies, will and should arise in any discussion about fundamental changes in our tax laws.

The second category, similar at least in concept to the first, would be a shift from our present tax on income to a tax on consumption. The base of a consumption tax would be determined in the same fashion as under the income tax, through individual tax returns at the end of each year, and the tax would be paid primarily through wage withholding. Whether or not that would in fact amount to a fundamental tax reform, given the number of credits and preferences for expenditure items in the present laws, may be open to question. But at least in theory it's a reform idea that appeals to some people.

The third and most frequently heard category of proposals for tax reform is the so-called flat tax or single-rate income tax. In its purest form it calls for a single rate of tax on all incomes less a fairly substantial personal exemption and deduction for any cost of doing business. As an elected member of the Congress, I can assure you that the desirability of a flat tax is the most frequent question on tax policy one gets from one's constituency. In the last year or two, I have never completed a service club speech on fiscal issues without having a question about the flat rate tax in the first three or four.

Enthusiasm for it among the average group of Rotarians disappears when they learn that to keep the present level of receipts many of them would pay more taxes than they do at the present time. This fact, however, does not by any means remove interest in the idea or in potential modifications of it.

The final proposed reform is the Bradley-Gephardt modification of the flat tax proposal. Their plan contains more mildly graduated tax rates than the present system and removes many but not all of the preferences in the tax code. Quite noticeable is the retention of deductions for interest on home mortgages and for charitable contributions. The difficulty with this proposal is that once you deviate from a purely flat tax and accept some deductions, credits, or exemptions, it's very difficult to decide where to stop.

Every single one of those preferences found its way into the tax code because it was the beloved child of some individual or some group at some place in the United States and was thought to have some social or economic utility. Consequently while a simplified and broader tax base is to be desired, it would not survive the legislative process and land on a president's desk in anything like the form in which it appears in the various reform proposals. Whether it would be recognizable at all is very much an open question.

Outlook

I'm inclined to think that in 1985, assuming Congress then will resemble the present Congress, there will be some significant changes in the tax code. The driving force of budget deficits, which will barely be affected by this year's down payment, makes that almost a necessity. The fact that we are not going to devastate the most fundamental of our spending priorities will require a broader tax base.

At the same time it is relatively safe to predict that we will not jump from our present system to a profoundly different system of taxation. Next year's changes are far more likely to be a close cousin to this year's changes, that is, they will be a further attack on loopholes or what are perceived to be loopholes. In addition there will almost certainly be a modest change in the present rate structure or some increase in excise taxation, though I don't think that we're within a year of a broadly based value-added tax. As was the case this year, new exemptions and preferences are likely to be created even when we are passing a bill designed to broaden the present tax system.

This is not to imply that the debate over fundamental reform will be fruitless. It will very likely have a significant effect on what takes place next year, just as it has had some effect on proposals this year.

The idea that, in a society as complex as ours, we are somehow going to move to a relatively simple tax system seems to me highly unlikely. We have gotten ourselves into the present situation for good and valid reasons, and future legislation will be subject to the same process and influenced by the same political forces. That does not mean that concern for tax reform by the business community and by the public at large is not important or vital. It is important and vital because it will chart the direction in which we move. But to expect perfection is to be inevitably subjected to disappointment, and to let the perfect be the enemy of the good is bad policy, from a social as well as fiscal point of view.

Can the Income Tax Continue to Be the Major Revenue Source?

MICHAEL J. GRAETZ

BEFORE I TURN to my principal mission here—evaluation of the present state of the federal income tax—I shall address briefly the question presented to me as fundamental by the organizers of this conference: can the income tax continue to be this country's major source of general revenue? In the first section below I answer that question in the affirmative. I then offer a detailed look at the ills of the income tax, beginning with the lingering problem of tax expenditures and proceeding to problems of the 1980s: inflation and compliance. After identifying problems common to reform of the current income tax and enactment of any coherent consumption tax, I conclude by asking whether the income tax *should* continue to be the principal source of revenue.

"Comparisons are odorous"[1]

If the income tax is not to remain this country's major revenue source, some other tax (or combination of taxes) must necessarily emerge as its replacement. The leading contender at the moment seems to be a broad-based tax on consumption, a tax which might take one of three forms: a retail sales tax, a value-added tax, or a personal progressive consumption tax, often labeled an expenditure tax.

A broad consumption-tax base is inherently smaller than a broad income-tax base. This fact is made clear by Henry Simons's famous definition of income as consumption plus accretions to wealth.[2] An income tax includes income in the base whether spent or saved; a consumption tax, in contrast, omits accretions from the base, taxing income only if spent. The same point may be illustrated by reference to the equality, under certain conditions, of a consumption base and a wage base.[3] A consumption tax is

---

1. William Shakespeare, *Much Ado About Nothing,* act 3, sc. 5, l. 18.
2. Henry C. Simons, *Personal Income Taxation,* vol. 50 (University of Chicago Press, 1938).
3. Michael J. Graetz, "Implementing a Progressive Consumption Tax," *Harvard Law Review,* vol. 92 (June 1979), pp. 1598–1609.

thus often said to exempt income from capital, whereas an income tax reaches both income from labor and from capital. Even under the Laffer curve, a zero rate of tax (in this case, on capital income)—unlike a low rate—raises no revenue. Since an income base is inherently broader than a consumption base, an income tax has the potential to raise more revenue at the same rates or to raise the same revenue at lower rates. Today, when the dominant economic factor influencing tax policy is the projection of very large current and future deficits, this seems no small advantage.

Two other factors may limit the revenue potential of a consumption tax: first, there would be no justification for any separate corporate tax (other than a withholding tax),[4] and second, unlike an income tax, it should be imposed on a tax-exclusive (as opposed to a tax-inclusive) base.[5] Today's top tax-inclusive income tax rate of 50 percent is equivalent to a tax-exclusive rate of 100 percent, and the pre-1981 top rate of 70 percent is equivalent to a tax-exclusive rate of 233⅓ percent. Notwithstanding their equivalence to currently accepted tax-inclusive rates, tax-exclusive rates of 100 percent or greater do not seem politically viable.

Including bequests and gifts in the tax base of the donor might enhance the revenue potential—as well as the fairness—of a consumption tax. This would be conceptually inconsistent with consumption tax principles, however, since the recipient, not the donor, would spend the bequest or gift. In any event, taxing bequests as consumption would seem to have little practical prospect of enactment in light of Congress's failure ever to enact a conceptually appropriate income tax on unrealized appreciation of assets held at death.

Consumption tax proponents sometimes urge that replacement of the income tax with a consumption tax be coupled with significant strengthening of estate and gift taxes or enactment of a wealth tax.[6] The revenue potential of a wealth transfer tax (such as an estate or gift tax) is quite limited, however; there is not enough wealth transferred annually for such a tax to raise a

4. Ibid., pp. 1634–42; American Bar Association, Section on Taxation, Committee on Simplification, "Complexity and the Personal Consumption Tax," *Tax Lawyer,* vol. 35 (Winter 1981–82), pp. 415, 437–39.

5. Graetz, "Implementing a Progressive Consumption Tax," pp. 1580–84; ABA, "Complexity and the Personal Consumption Tax," pp. 431–33.

6. See, for example, John Stewart Mill, *Principles of Political Economy* (Laughlin, 1884); Nicholas Kaldor, *An Expenditure Tax* (London: Allen and Unwin, 1955); William D. Andrews, "A Consumption-Type or Cash Flow Personal Income Tax," *Harvard Law Review,* vol. 87 (April 1974), pp. 1113–19.

significant portion of federal revenues. Moreover, taxation of bequests is extremely unpopular politically.[7]

A periodic low-rate wealth tax, which could raise substantial revenues without imposing high marginal rates on income from capital, has not received serious attention in this country, although its use is widespread in Europe. A wealth tax is viewed widely (though wrongly, I believe) as impractical because of valuation and liquidity problems; in addition, a wealth tax would be a "direct" tax that could not serve as a source of federal revenue without a constitutional amendment or a constitutionally effective disguise.

The foregoing paragraphs do not deny the substantial revenue potential of broad-based consumption taxes as supplements to or partial replacements for the income tax. Instead, they are intended to emphasize that to substitute a consumption tax for the income tax would be to choose a base that is inherently narrower due to the omission of savings. The revenue question might well look quite different if the income tax were to be replaced by a combination of consumption and wealth taxes or even by a consumption tax that included bequests in the decedent's final consumption tax return. No such combination appears likely, however, given that much of the support for a consumption tax is attributable to its alleged advantages over the income tax in stimulating capital formation and economic growth and the practical and political barriers to taxing bequests or wealth.

The question whether the income tax can remain this nation's major source of general revenue can therefore be answered in the negative only if the income tax is in such a state of disrepair that its demise is both imminent and inevitable. My evaluation suggests that, although the current income tax has some serious troubles, this is not the case. This discussion of the relative revenue potential of income and consumption taxes identifies the critical issue in an evaluation of the income tax: how well does the income tax serve in taxing income from capital and how well might it serve? Before turning to that question, however, I shall briefly discuss practical politics.

A word on practical politics

Tax reform is one of those apple pie issues—everybody seems for it. All agree on the need to simplify the tax laws, produce greater equity among taxpayers, and promote economic efficiency and

7. See Michael J. Graetz, "To Praise The Estate Tax, Not To Bury It," *Yale Law Journal,* vol. 93 (December 1983), pp. 259–86.

growth. But general goals are far easier to embrace than specific legislation. Congressional capacity to deal with major tax reform legislation has long been subject to criticism. The Tax Reform Act of 1969, for example, prompted syndicated columnist Joseph Kraft to remark: "It is now clear that taxes are too complicated and sensitive a matter to be decided in detail by the Congress. . . . The Congress in fiscal matters is a dinosaur—huge body and tiny brain."[8]

Unfortunately, things have gotten worse: prospects for structural tax reform have been dimmed by recent "reforms" in congressional practices; public pressure to enact income tax reforms seems nonexistent; political leadership on tax matters has become increasingly diffuse; committee deliberations are now open to the public and are well attended by representatives of groups with a special interest in the outcome; and political action committees now have great influence in guiding policy decisions. In short, for those who would urge massive tax reforms, there is more than ample cause for despair.

This political reality suggests that change, if it comes at all, will necessarily come gradually and incrementally. Neither comprehensive income taxes nor comprehensive consumption taxes are likely to be enacted overnight. It is singularly inappropriate to contrast the current income tax with an ideal consumption tax, since politics inhibits the prospects for ideal taxation regardless of whether the base is income or consumption. To believe that Congress can enact an ideal consumption tax but cannot fix the current income tax is to believe that both ends of a seesaw can be up at the same time.

In fact, many of the priorities for broadening the tax base would be the same under a comprehensive consumption tax as under the income tax. For example, current income tax rules that permit many taxpayers to enjoy tax-free personal consumption (for example, by excluding compensatory fringe benefits or deducting consumption-laden business expenses) would be as unacceptable under a consumption tax as they are under the income tax. Indeed, such exclusions seem even less acceptable under a consumption tax, especially if a consumption tax requires higher rates because of its inherently narrower base. The political and administrative difficulties of appropriately including such items in the tax base would not be diminished under a consumption tax.

By the same token, the income tax and the consumption tax

8. Joseph Kraft, "Power to Destroy," *Washington Post,* December 7, 1969.

raise essentially identical issues with respect to most itemized deductions (such as those for charitable contributions, medical expenses, and state and local taxes) and many exclusions from income (such as imputed rents on owner-occupied homes, government transfers, prizes and awards, and scholarships and fellowships). And deductions of interest payments for home mortgages and other consumer loans would be inappropriate under a consumption tax. These difficult issues would not disappear by shifting from income to expenditure taxation and would continue to depend upon policy objectives extrinsic to the design of a comprehensive tax base.

Tax reform might usefully begin with legislation that would be appropriate to either a broad-based income or consumption tax. Such an approach would postpone differences between advocates of income and consumption taxes and might raise substantial revenues for reducing deficits or lowering tax rates.

Old business: tax expenditures

One of the great services of Richard Goode's paper for this conference is his demonstration of the longevity of most tax preference provisions and his attribution of the recent increases in the tax expenditure budget to greater use of old provisions.[9] Goode found that more than 80 percent of the estimated revenue cost of tax expenditures in fiscal year 1982 derived from provisions thirty-five years old and that 95 percent derived from provisions enacted before 1970. The "tax expenditure" label and budget estimation of their revenue cost may be creatures of the late 1960s, but the preferential provisions themselves are of long standing.

I will not again rehearse the discussion of tax expenditure provisions that so fills the tax policy literature. Rather, I will address briefly two issues that seem especially relevant to the current context: (1) tax expenditures under a consumption tax and (2) income tax preferences for retirement savings. The related problem of tax shelter investments will be considered in connection with my discussion of inflation.

The Prospects for Tax Expenditures under a Consumption Tax

As I indicated above, many of the tax preference provisions now listed in the tax expenditure budget would present essentially identical issues under a consumption tax. The elimination of savings from the consumption tax base would in theory eliminate any need for differential treatment of different kinds of investment.

9. Richard Goode, "Lessons from Seven Decades of Income Taxation," this volume.

Purchases of investment assets would be immediately deductible under an expenditure tax; such cash-flow treatment can be viewed as equivalent to an exemption of yield from these assets, so that there would be no tax on investment income. A negative rate of tax would be required to create tax advantages for favored investments; but negative tax rates are not unknown even under the income tax, and consumption tax preferences for particular investments would be easy to implement as a technical matter. The comments of an American Bar Association committee seem apt:

> The forces that have led to differential treatment that is avoidable under the income tax are unlikely to disappear with the adoption of a consumption tax. . . .
>
> We do not . . . agree that there would necessarily be less differential treatment under one tax than the other. Differences due to arbitrary income tax conventions such as depreciation rates may diminish under the consumption tax, but deliberate differences would seem as possible under one tax as the other. The income tax has been in existence for over half a century and is, in part, the result of the successful efforts of special pleaders. We see no reason to believe that those interested in preferential treatment would be less effective in the lawmaking process if the standard of equal treatment became consumption rather than income. Nor are we convinced that zero is a natural lower bound on effective tax rates, below which those seeking preferential treatment would necessarily be unsuccessful.[10]

Income Tax Preferences for Retirement Savings

One advantage claimed for the consumption tax over the income tax is its more favorable treatment of the choice to postpone consumption. The current income tax, however, already contains a variety of preferences for retirement savings; the most notable of these are for qualified deferred pension and profit-sharing plans and individual retirement accounts, which together with home ownership constitute the principal form of savings for many middle-income taxpayers. Investment income earned by such plans or accounts should be taxed under a theoretically appropriate comprehensive income tax. In fact, the existing advantages for retirement savings contribute significantly to the notion that the current income tax is a hybrid—part income tax, part consumption tax.

This is not an occasion to treat the issue of savings for retirement in any more detail than to applaud this particular income "tax

10. ABA, "Complexity and the Personal Consumption Tax," pp. 433–34.

expenditure." A progressive income tax will naturally tend to impose its greatest burden in an individual's high-earning years, typically the middle years. Generous income tax provisions for tax-free accumulation of retirement savings, while still placing the highest tax burden in the highest earning years, provide a useful lifetime averaging effect and mitigate significantly the natural income tax preference for present over deferred consumption. A tax on consumption, in contrast, will tend to impose relatively heavier burdens in the high-consumption, low-earning years of youth and old age.

Today's income tax problems: inflation and compliance

The problem of income tax expenditures is old business: a problem whose solutions are generally well known although difficult to enact without political leadership and will. In contrast, the problems of inflation and compliance constitute new business: substantial problems whose impact and solutions remain uncertain.

Inflation

The current income tax structure was designed for a world of stable prices. The past decade of unexpected and fluctuating inflation rates has produced bizarre patterns of both undertaxation and overtaxation, particularly with respect to capital and income from capital. I now believe that the federal income tax must be systematically restructured to deal with inflation. My opinion, however, is not yet widely accepted. Proposals for comprehensive income taxation, including the 1983 Bradley-Gephardt bill (S. 1421), routinely ignore the problem of inflation. These efforts to reform the income tax while ignoring inflation are simply 1960s solutions to 1980s problems.

There are three ways in which unexpected and fluctuating rates of inflation seriously affect the income tax. Two of these are well recognized: "bracket creep" and the distorted measurement of income from capital. The third is the increased importance of timing.

Bracket creep. Inflation distorts the dollar amounts specified in the Internal Revenue Code and the progressive rate structure. In the Economic Recovery Tax Act of 1981, Congress finally dealt with bracket creep by enacting indexing provisions scheduled to become effective in 1985. The failure to respond to this problem sooner, however, has taken its toll on the income tax. Citizens have come to question the fairness of the tax after repeatedly paying higher marginal tax rates on the same level of real income. Moreover, subjecting more and more taxpayers to higher marginal rates has increased the revenues lost as a result of tax expenditure provisions and made more significant structural distortions in the measurement of income.

Distorted measurement of capital income. The second way inflation distorts the income tax is through its widespread mismeasurement of net income; the mismeasurement occurs by offsetting the amounts spent or incurred in an earlier year's dollars against income received or earned in a subsequent year's dollars. These well-known distortions in measuring income from capital principally affect capital gains and losses, depreciation allowances, accounting for inventories, and the tax treatment of debt, particularly misallocations between interest and principal. A systematic response to these problems has been eschewed by Congress as well as by academic and professional observers. The income tax has instead been subjected to a variety of "solutions," such as the 1978 expansion of the capital gains exclusion and the 1981 acceleration of depreciation deductions; this tinkering has produced incentives for the inefficient allocation of resources by imposing widely divergent tax rates across industries and among companies in the same industry. Meanwhile, problems of inflation with respect to debt have largely been ignored on the theory that undertaxation of debtors will somehow in the aggregate be compensated for by overtaxation of creditors.

Congress's priorities in responding to the overtaxation of assets yielding capital income no doubt reflects the attitude of its constituents. Its delay in dealing with the overtaxation of lenders results from its recognition of the simultaneous obligation to redress the undertaxation of the many more numerous borrowers. Moreover, taxable institutional lenders, such as banks and insurance companies, can shelter much of their overstated income, and tax-exempt lenders, such as pension funds and university endowment funds, are indifferent to income overstatement. Influential commentators have contributed to the imbalance: lawyers have pointed to the practical difficulties of income tax indexing, with emphasis on the special problems of indexing debt, and economists have confirmed the priority of asset adjustment over debt by focusing on the inhibiting effect of asset overtaxation on capital formation.

The failure of Congress to revise the taxation of debt to account for inflation, together with its capriciousness in revising the taxation of assets, has created an income tax that is incapable of measuring the income of asset owners, debtors, or creditors.

Because Polonius' admonition to refrain from borrowing or lending is universally ignored in modern American society, this means that the wrong tax burden has been imposed on virtually every individual and corporation.

The current income tax rules, developed in response to inflation, can fairly be characterized as imposing a zero rate of tax on the income from important categories of assets. These include investments in tax-exempt state and local bonds; equipment, which can essentially be immediately expensed by a combination of accelerated cost recovery deductions and the investment tax credit; natural resource exploration and development, where immediate expensing is generally permitted; real estate, which often produces negative income tax rates; retirement savings, as detailed earlier; and all assets held by tax-exempt organizations or taxable corporations with large operating losses. Harvey Galper and Eugene Steuerle have recently estimated that as much as 80 percent of the $10.5 trillion of assets held by individuals qualifies for such favored treatment.[11]

Two sets of problems, both labeled tax arbitrage, have resulted. First, the income tax produces great incentives for undertaxed assets to be held by taxpayers subject to the highest marginal rates and for overtaxed assets, such as loans that produce taxable interest, to be held by low-bracket taxpayers and tax-exempt entities. Structural provisions of the Internal Revenue Code, designed for a simpler era, allow transactions to be planned so as to maximize arbitrage opportunities and thereby to achieve large tax savings. Innovative tax-planning devices, such as zero-coupon bonds, equipment and real estate leasing by loss corporations and tax-exempt organizations, and family sale and leaseback transactions, have become commonplace. The tax distinction between being a lender and an owner has assumed overwhelming importance in the allocation of tax burdens and benefits at the same time that its already tenuous economic and legal distinctions have been blurred by new lending practices, especially equity participations.

In addition, nonsystematic tax reductions to compensate for inflation have created enormous new advantages for selecting one form of legal entity over another. For example, there have been

---

11. Harvey Galper and Eugene Steuerle, "Tax Incentives for Savings," *Brookings Review*, vol. 2 (Winter 1983), pp. 19–20.

efforts to take advantage of the rules of entity taxation by structuring transactions through large or even publicly owned limited partnerships and by spinning off corporate assets into royalty trusts. These rules further enhance opportunities to shift undertaxed income and deductions to high-bracket taxpayers, while shifting other income in the opposite direction. Congress has generally responded by floundering, a prime example of which is its recent enactments dealing with leasing of depreciable assets. Commentators have offered little help, often treating deep structural problems as if they were necessary complements to congressional decisions to provide tax preferences for certain kinds of investments.

A related problem, also labeled tax arbitrage, occurs when the same taxpayer simultaneously engages in debt and asset transactions where the asset is eligible for favored income tax treatment. Taxpayers can achieve a negative tax rate overall when they can obtain both an interest deduction and the equivalent of a zero tax rate on the asset transaction. Other income tax rules (such as the *Crane* rule[12]) may produce "conversion" by significantly expanding the deductions allowable against ordinary income under circumstances where the recoupment of those deductions will be taxed as capital gain, if at all. As Richard Goode has pointed out, this form of tax arbitrage is very common, occurring not only in the case of highly publicized tax shelters but whenever individuals have homes financed by mortgages or a combination of debt and tax-preferred retirement savings. Congress has only on rare occasion denied interest deductions—as under sections 163(d) and 265(2) of the Internal Revenue Code—in order to narrow the gap between deductible interest and full or partial exemption of capital income. Other congressional, judicial, and administrative efforts to constrict the use of borrowing to expand deductions have likewise been limited responses to abuse cases; examples include the at-risk rules of section 465; the contingent debt cases, such as *Gibson Products*;[13] and the overvaluation cases such as *Estate of Franklin*.[14]

Timing. The third important effect of inflation on the income tax is to magnify dramatically the significance of timing issues.

---

12. *Crane* v. *Commissioner*, 331 U.S. 1 (1947).

13. *Gibson Products Co.* v. *United States*, 637 F.2d 101 (5th Cir. 1981). Contingent nature of obligation prevents inclusion in basis of oil and gas leases of nonrecourse debt secured by leases, drilling equipment, and percentage of future production.

14. *Estate of Franklin* v. *Commissioner*, 544 F.2d 1045 (9th Cir. 1976). Basis does not include mortgage where loan is significantly in excess of fair market value of the property.

High interest rates, which have been correlated with inflation, have raised substantially the tax stakes of allocating deductions to earlier taxable years and income to later taxable years. In labeling issues of income tax timing as "trivial" in 1938, Henry Simons clearly marked himself as a man before our time. Even in more recent years, Congress has seemed to concur in that judgment, routinely justifying decisions to accelerate deductions or to delay income recognition as "only a matter of timing." The distinction between life and death is also only a matter of timing.

The belated nature of concern for income tax timing issues is nowhere better evidenced than by the fact that it was not until 1982 that Congress seemed to discover compound interest. The Tax Equity and Fiscal Responsibility Act of 1982 required, for the first time, compounding of interest on tax underpayments and measurement of interest income on bonds originally issued at a discount.

At least one consumption tax proponent, William D. Andrews, seems to regard timing issues as the fundamental reason to abandon the income tax in favor of consumption taxation. He has termed the realization requirement the "Achilles' heel" of the income tax.[15] The theoretically proper consumption tax solution to timing issues is to postpone taxation of savings until consumed and thereby to make the measurement of income for any particular year relatively unimportant. Under a consumption tax, deferral provisions, roundly criticized under the income tax, would simply be extended to all investments. The quest for taxing capital income would be abandoned largely on the assertion that such income cannot be measured for purposes of income taxation.

The more conservative course would first systematically review current timing issues in an effort to delineate significant problems of economic efficiency or tax equity and then attempt to restructure the income tax to resolve those problems. Such a reexamination will require a fresh look at well-accepted and long-unquestioned principles of tax accounting as well as at rules governing the timing of recovery of basis of assets. Moreover, if recent tax straddle arrangements and hedging transactions with stock options are, as I suspect, merely the tip of a very deep iceberg, critical scrutiny of the decision to tax only realized gains and losses will also be necessary.

15. William D. Andrews, "The Achilles' Heel of the Comprehensive Income Tax," in Charles E. Walker and Mark A. Bloomfield, eds., *New Directions in Federal Tax Policy for the 1980s* (Ballinger, 1983), pp. 278–85.

Study also seems required to determine whether all timing issues can really be expected to disappear under a consumption tax. If, for example, a corporate tax based on flow of funds or cash flow were to be coupled with a personal consumption tax, as many consumption tax proponents have urged, the cash method of accounting would be required of all businesses. No consumption tax advocate has yet addressed the complexity that would result from such tax requirements or the problems that might emerge if, as under the current income tax, both cash and accrual accounts were permitted depending on the business's method of book accounting; nor has any such advocate given the reasons that prescription of a single tax accounting method would be politically possible under a consumption tax but not under an income tax.

As the foregoing suggests, unpredictable and fluctuating inflation rates of the past decade have taken a substantial toll on the income tax. To date, Congress has refused to address systematically the resulting problems of timing or tax-base measurement. This income tax tinkering, in lieu of systematic inflation adjustment, has produced business income tax burdens that vary widely among individuals, industries, and businesses within the same industry depending upon their investment, financing, or accounting practices. An income tax that produces such wide and inconsistent variations in tax burdens is readily subject to criticism on grounds of tax justice as well as economic efficiency and growth. Yet, all of the proposals for comprehensive income tax reform currently before Congress have ignored the problems that result from the fluctuating and unexpected inflation rates that have become a fact of economic life in the United States. The income tax must systematically deal with this fact if it is to remain this country's major source of revenue. A consumption tax may indeed become inevitable if the alternative is continued tinkering with the income tax that maintains an irrational and indefensible mix of overtaxation and undertaxation.

The Rise in Tax Shelter Investments

The failure to adjust the income tax base for inflation has significantly contributed to the proliferation of tax-shelter investments by routinely permitting an individual to achieve negative income tax rates. This is accomplished by combining undertaxed borrowing with accelerated deductions or income postponements or exclusions, adopted either to encourage particular investments or to offset overtaxation of capital income in inflationary times. This regime has, of course, created incentives for certain investments, whether or not economically viable, and produced after-tax profits on investments that produce little or no profit before tax. No doubt the increasingly widespread appeal of tax-shelter investments is also attributable to bracket creep from inflation and to the anti-income-tax attitudes that Richard Goode also associates with inflation.

The problem has been further amplified by the inability of the Internal Revenue Service to police even those tax-shelter investments that have no adequate basis in law or fact. The IRS has conducted too few audits and has only recently acquired the computer capability to identify tax-shelter problems. Attorneys have readily provided "fraud insurance" through tax-shelter opinion letters and, until recently, the sanction structure was such that even those taxpayers whose tax-shelter deductions were disallowed by the IRS still obtained, assuming no fraud penalty, the equivalent of a below-market loan from the government without the effect on financial statements or the messy paperwork required by other institutional lenders. The compliance provisions of the 1982 tax legislation will help somewhat to constrict the profusion of abusive tax-shelter investments.

One of the major advantages attributed to a consumption tax is its reduction or elimination of tax-sheltered investments. Of course, it is impossible to envision what new shelters might be devised under a consumption tax;[16] nevertheless, a few observations can be offered.

Tax-shelter investments typically have at least one of three elements that contribute to tax reduction: (1) *deferral* of tax through acceleration of deductions or postponement of income; (2) *conversion*, which results from deducting from ordinary income the expenses of investments whose income, if taxable at all, will be taxed at lower rates (capital-gain rates, for example); and (3) *leverage*, which increases deferral and conversion by increasing deductible amounts and, through interest deductions, often produces negative tax rates.

Deferral. The consumption tax would eliminate the deferral advantages of tax shelters—that is, the acceleration of deductions that should properly be taken in later years—but only by accelerating the deduction of all investment expenses. The income tax

---

16. As the ABA Tax Simplification Committee suggests: "We cannot possibly foresee the potential for 'consumption tax shelters' that might develop in the future. Surely no one in 1913 could have foreseen the income tax shelters that came into existence in the 1960s and 1970s." ABA, "Complexity and the Personal Consumption Tax," p. 435.

aberration, therefore, becomes the consumption tax norm and is no longer an odious shelter.

Conversion. As indicated above, a consumption tax implies a zero tax on all income from capital. This is expected to eliminate any need for special capital-gain rates or other capital-income exclusions or preferences and thus provide no opportunity for conversion. Under an income tax, conversion could be reduced or eliminated by taxing capital gains in the same manner as ordinary income, by extending capitalization or recapture rules, or by disallowing deductions associated with capital-gain income.

Leverage. The great advantage of a properly implemented consumption tax over the current income tax with respect to tax shelters would be in reducing tax-shelter opportunities available through borrowing. Disallowing interest deductions would be a substantial improvement over the current income tax situation, but implementing a consumption tax on cash flow principles would have the additional effect of preventing borrowing from increasing taxpayers' investment deductions beyond their equity investment. A similar rule could be adopted under the current income tax, but this would require reversing the longstanding rule of *Crane* v. *Commissioner*.[17] Some inroads have recently been made on the *Crane* doctrine, such as disallowing deductions where loans are nonrecourse, where loans exceed the related assets' value, and where repayment is considered unduly contingent, and further inroads are possible even under the income tax.

It seems disingenuous to expect that special interests, such as the real estate industry, would prove any less resistant under a consumption tax than under the current income tax to the enactment of restrictions on deductions attributable to borrowed funds. Again, the alleged advantages of the consumption tax appear to turn on the dubious assumption that changes that are politically impossible under an income tax could be easily achieved under a consumption tax.

In 1973, Secretary of the Treasury George P. Shultz proposed a "limitation on artificial losses" provision that would have restricted tax-shelter opportunities by preventing deductions from tax-shelter investments from offsetting unrelated income.[18] This approach now is found in the minimum tax rules that limit interest deductions and in rules for so-called hobby losses and vacation

17. *Crane* v. *Commissioner*, 331 U.S. 1 (1947).
18. See *General Tax Reform*, Hearings before House Committee on Ways and Means, 93 Cong. 1 sess. (GPO, 1973), pt. 16, pp. 6985–86.

homes. Thus, an appropriate income tax response to the general problem of tax-shelter investments has been known for at least a decade; it simply awaits enactment.

The Role of the Corporate Income Tax

A few years back, Lily Tomlin played the lead role in an abominable movie called *The Incredible Shrinking Woman*. In terms of national tax policy, the corporate income tax has been playing a similar role in an equally bad entertainment. In 1953, the corporate income tax accounted for 27.8 percent of federal revenue and 5.3 percent of gross national product. By 1980, immediately before the most recent liberalization of depreciation allowances, the revenue produced by the corporate tax had halved as a percentage of both total federal revenues and GNP. In 1983, the corporate tax was estimated to account for only 9.3 percent of federal revenues and 1.8 percent of GNP. No estimate of future revenues expects the corporate tax to produce more than about 10 percent of federal revenues. It is no wonder that Secretary of the Treasury Donald Regan could remark that the 1981 legislation had essentially repealed the corporate income tax on new investments. The individual income tax, by contrast, has accounted for a relatively steady percentage of federal revenue and GNP over the past thirty years: 46.0 percent of federal revenue and 8.8 percent of GNP in 1953 as compared with 45.9 percent of revenue and 8.9 percent of GNP in 1983.[19]

In theory, if an income tax is imposed on individuals, a corporate income tax is necessary only to ensure that undistributed corporate income does not escape tax. This suggests that the current corporate income tax should be criticized for taxing corporate earnings distributed to shareholders as dividends more heavily than other kinds of individual income, since these earnings are subject to tax at both the corporate and shareholder levels. By the same token, undistributed corporate earnings are improperly taxed whenever corporate tax rates differ from the rates of its shareholders. Corporate earnings distributed to lenders as interest are deductible and therefore escape the corporate-level tax. It is evident from this perspective that the theoretically proper reform of the corporate income tax would be to repeal the separate corporate tax and attribute undistributed corporate income directly

19. Data for 1953, *The National Income and Product Accounts of the United States, 1929–76, Statistical Tables*, Supplement to the *Survey of Current Business* (GPO, 1981), pp. 1, 123. For 1980 and 1983, *Survey of Current Business*, vol. 62 (July 1982), pp. 22, 47–48; vol. 64 (May 1984), pp. 4, 7.

to shareholders for taxation at their marginal rates. Any remaining corporate tax would be only a withholding tax that would be credited to shareholders as corporate income was distributed or attributed to them.

Many commentators, however, have deemed impractical the imputation and taxation to shareholders of retained corporate earnings. They have urged, as a second-best solution, the repeal of the corporate tax on earnings distributed to shareholders as dividends.[20] This change would be accomplished by phasing-in either a corporate deduction for dividends or a shareholder credit for corporate taxes paid. Corporate managers, however, have resisted such proposals, preferring that corporate tax reductions be focused on retained, rather than distributed, earnings. Toward this end, they have advanced, with the concurrence of the economics profession, bang-for-the-buck arguments regarding the likely impact of corporate tax reductions as an investment stimulus. As a result, both dividend relief and corporate rate reductions have been rejected in favor of investment credits and liberalized depreciation allowances.

Depreciation allowances were increased in 1954, 1962, 1971, and 1981; further increases for 1985 and 1986, enacted in 1981, were repealed in 1982. The investment credit was enacted in 1962, suspended in 1966, reinstated in 1967, permanently repealed in 1969, permanently reinstated in 1971, increased in 1975, revised in 1981, and reduced in 1982.

Needless to say, these tax changes have not been systematically calibrated to produce similar corporate tax burdens across industries. Alan J. Auerbach has recently estimated effective corporate tax rates to range from a low of 6.3 percent for the water transportation industry to a high of 39.4 percent for the industry composed of water supply, sanitary services, and certain utilities. Wholesale trade corporations are subject to an estimated 18.7 percent corporate tax rate; retail trade corporations, 27.5 percent.[21] One would be hard pressed indeed to explain these widely varying rates as a reflection of congressional priorities for the allocation of resources. At the company (as opposed to the industry) level, corporate tax rates show even wider divergence depending both on the company's previous pattern of gains and losses (which may, in turn, depend upon previous depreciation advantages or

20. See, for example, Charles E. McLure, Jr., *Must Corporate Income Be Taxed Twice?* (Brookings Institution, 1979).

21. Alan J. Auerbach, "Corporate Taxation in the United States," *Brookings Papers on Economic Activity, 2:1983,* p. 468.

disadvantages) and on its financing patterns, particularly the relationship between debt and equity financing. The ability to file consolidated returns, which permit tax losses from one business to offset tax gains from others, creates further variations in tax burdens between conglomerate and unintegrated companies. This patchwork of corporate tax rules produces enormous misallocations of resources within the corporate sector. While I am always skeptical of such estimates, Auerbach has estimated that differential corporate taxation resulted in 1981 in the waste of 3.19 percent of the net corporate capital stock of $2.05 trillion dollars, or more than $65 billion dollars of capital. His estimates for 1982 are significantly lower because of the basis reduction for investment tax credits that was enacted that year.[22]

As indicated previously, much of the waste is due to the way in which Congress has haphazardly attempted to correct for inflation-related distortions of the income tax base. The tax regime of recent years has moved debt toward high-rate taxpayers and credit toward low- or zero-rate taxpayers as they attempt to take advantage of the asymmetries in the taxation of assets and loans. Related transactions to compensate for differential taxation, for example, equipment and real estate leasing by government agencies and tax-exempt organizations, provide ample evidence that tax planning is a dynamic process.

Moreover, the failure to adjust tax rules systematically to reflect inflation has further exacerbated the structural preference for debt over equity finance in the United States classical corporate income tax. But the government has repeatedly proved incapable of writing rules readily distinguishing between debt and equity.

This brief survey makes clear the appropriate remedies for the corporate income tax: assets and debt alike should be indexed to compensate for inflation. The corporate-level tax on earnings distributed to shareholders as dividends should be phased out. Depreciation allowances and corporate tax rates could then be adjusted to provide rates that are more uniform both across and within industries and that are consistent with revenue and investment goals for the corporate sector. If these structural reforms prove politically impossible, the current inequities and inefficiencies could be largely reduced by totally or partially disallowing corporate interest deductions while totally or partially excluding from income interest received from corporations.

The important issue of corporate losses would remain to be

22. Ibid., p. 471.

addressed. The current tax pressures for mergers could be relieved either by making such losses more transferable or by restricting their ability to offset income from unrelated activity.

It would be unnecessary to allocate undistributed corporate income to shareholders under an expenditure tax because such a tax would attach only when that income was devoted to consumption. To the extent that the taxation of business is regarded as complementary to the taxation of individuals, the adoption of a consumption tax at the individual level would imply the elimination of taxes on business income: businesses are engaged in production, not consumption. Corporate earnings retained for additional investment should be exempt from tax, as should amounts invested and saved by individuals. Investors should generally be allowed deductions for purchases of corporate stock; they should be taxed similarly on all cash receipts resulting from stock ownership, whether received as dividends, return of capital, or proceeds from the sale of stock.

Most proponents of expenditure taxation would prefer to retain a separate corporate tax, usually in the form of a cash flow tax. I am skeptical of cash flow corporate tax proposals because they essentially would make the government an automatic joint venturer in all corporate endeavors without granting it the participation in management generally accorded to important joint venturers. Of course, if the government were to become such a joint participant, it might then feel less constrained to eschew a commensurate role in corporate decisionmaking. If such proposals are advanced merely to prohibit windfall gains on old investments, better alternatives are likely to be available. It should also be noted that the issue of losses would continue to be important under a cash flow corporate tax.

Tax Compliance Problems

No effort to discuss the income tax today would be complete without at least cursory examination of compliance problems. A large revenue gap, estimated to be in the range of $100 billion and growing, has resulted from a combination of unreported income and overstated deductions.[23]

Our theoretical and factual knowledge of the compliance problem is in the fledgling stage. The economics-based literature on crime and punishment has made little progress since the basic

23. See, for example, *Tax Compliance Act of 1982 and Related Legislation,* Hearings before the House Committee on Ways and Means, 97 Cong. 2 sess. (GPO, 1982).

theoretical structure was established fifteen years ago by Gary S. Becker.[24] In that framework, criminal activity is treated as a rational decision based upon probabilities of detection and conviction and levels of punishment. Economists have on several occasions applied these models to tax evasion and avoidance.[25] The Tax Equity and Fiscal Responsibility Act of 1982 seems to embrace the basic posture of the economics of crime literature, describing the tax collection process as a "tax or audit lottery" and employing a variety of techniques designed to narrow the so-called compliance gap; these techniques include budget increases for law enforcement efforts, new and increased civil and criminal sanctions, and new withholding and reporting requirements. In fact, these compliance measures were expected to raise one-third of the total revenue to be raised by the 1982 legislation.

Unfortunately, most of the theoretical work to date is not particularly useful for either policy analysis or empirical study. The most significant reason for this shortcoming is that the models simply do not reflect real-world legal or administrative structures or the costs of achieving improved compliance. Current models also ignore possible effects of group interactions, even though increased noncompliance by one group of taxpayers is widely expected to influence the behavior of others.

Empirical uncertainties also abound. James S. Henry, who has conducted the most comprehensive survey to date of federal income tax noncompliance, has cast serious doubt on the methodological soundness of all of the half-dozen or so empirical studies contained in the literature.[26] Nevertheless, conservative estimates suggest that unreported taxable income has averaged 10–15 percent of total taxable income in recent years, and IRS commissioners seem convinced that the rate of noncompliance has been growing dramatically. IRS Commissioner Roscoe L. Egger, Jr., reported that the "income tax gap" created by revenues lost from legal sources of income grew from $29 billion in 1973 to $87 billion in 1981 and, without the 1982 legislation, was

---

24. Gary S. Becker, "Crime and Punishment: An Economic Approach," *Journal of Political Economy,* vol. 76 (March–April 1968), pp. 169–217.

25. See, for example, Michael G. Allingham and Agnar Sandmo, "Income Tax Evasion: A Theoretical Analysis," *Journal of Public Economics,* vol. 1 (November 1972), pp. 323–38.

26. James S. Henry, "Noncompliance With U.S. Tax Law: Evidence on Size, Growth, and Composition," *Income Tax Compliance: A Report of the ABA Section on Taxation Invitational Conference on Income Tax Compliance* (Chicago: American Bar Association, 1983), pp. 15–112.

expected to grow to $120 billion in 1985.[27] Shocking estimates are also offered of income tax evasion in the illegal sector. The compliance gap has become a justification not only for new enforcement measures but also for major substantive proposals. The latter include significant reductions of tax rates and the replacement of income taxation with consumption taxation, which is often said to produce fewer compliance problems.

It is my view that compliance problems are serious indeed. Further legislative and administrative attention to the problem is virtually certain, especially as tax increases are required to narrow the deficit. We are in desperate need of richer theoretical models and further empirical investigation. The existing evidence suggests, however, that major changes in tax rates or the tax base are unlikely to result in improved compliance.

The most surprising fact that emerges from the theoretical models and the relevant tax law is that *anyone* complied with the income tax law in the past decade whenever fraud penalties could have been avoided. The most rudimentary cost-benefit analysis of a decision whether or not to underreport taxable income reveals the following characteristic: if the sanction structure is to have any deterrent effect, a probability of punishment of less than 100 percent requires that the sanction must be greater than the amount of the cheater's benefit. During the past decade, while aggregate audit probabilities were typically closer to 2 percent than 100 percent, interest rates on understated tax liabilities were often less than market rates. The sanction and detection structure has been so lenient toward underreporting that the high compliance rate can only be explained by taxpayers' (and third-party reporters') commitment to the responsibilities of citizenship and respect for the law. The 1981 and 1982 legislation has begun to reverse this imbalance, but the income tax can still be viewed as a game that favors significantly those who underreport. The compliance problem will not be solved if we merely lower tax rates or modify the tax base without addressing the structural issues of detection and punishment.

In fact, the notion that lowering tax rates will induce greater compliance is supported neither by the theory of tax compliance nor by the empirical evidence. This notion stems, at least in part, from the basic cost-benefit calculation that underreporting produces lesser benefits at lower rates of tax. Where fraud penalties are not applicable, however, lower tax rates will also reduce the

27. *Tax Compliance Act of 1982,* p. 5.

costs of underreporting, and the cost-benefit calculation will remain unchanged. When the basic economic model is revised to include government auditing and collection agents as a factor in the tax compliance calculus, lowering rates might even suggest greater, rather than lesser, noncompliance.[28]

The emerging mythology that noncompliance would be solved by replacing the income tax with a personal tax on consumption is not supported by examination of the sources of noncompliance. With respect to illegal sources of income, personal consumption taxes are not likely to prove any easier to collect than personal income taxes. With regard to legal income sources, most underreporting has historically involved sources of income, such as tips, subject neither to withholding nor to effective information reporting. It seems therefore that the underreporting of receipts from labor and capital would be as great a problem under a consumption tax as it is under the income tax. Enforcement will tend to depend upon the efficacy of withholding, third-party reporting and information-gathering mechanisms, and the ability of the IRS to match third-party information with individual returns. A closer look at two important sources of unreported income, tips and capital gains, should make this clear. Consider the following March 1984 National Public Radio report on an anonymous New York waitress:

> "You know, I have nothing against the government, they need the money too."
>
> That is a waitress, she works here in New York City, at a not very nice restaurant. She told me that she does not report any of her tips at tax time. The Treasury Department meanwhile, in Washington, has estimated that up to 84 percent of tip income has gone unreported. . .
>
> I asked my waitress what was her salary. How much did she make?
> "I get a buck fifty-five an hour."
>
> Reporter: A buck fifty-five an hour, on the understanding that's not really what you are getting?
>
> Waitress: "Oh no, you think I'd work for $1.55 an hour?"
>
> Reporter: You don't look like the kind of person who'd work for $1.55 an hour. (ha, ha.) What do you do with the cash when they give it to you? . . .
>
> My waitress [said] that she puts her unreported income in the bank every Monday:

28. Michael J. Graetz, Jennifer F. Reinganum, and Louis L. Wilde, "An Equilibrium Model of Tax Compliance With a Baysian Auditor and Some 'Honest' Taxpayers" (forthcoming); Michael J. Graetz, Jennifer F. Reinganum, and Louis L. Wilde, "A Model of Tax Compliance Under Budget-Constrained Auditors" (forthcoming).

"Oh yeah, I put it in the bank, what else am I going to do with it?"

Reporter: Well do you have any fear that little you, a waitress somewhere in the city of New York, would be noticed by the Internal Revenue Service and caught?

Waitress: "I bank the money, I don't spend it very much."

Reporter: But there it is. It's on file. Your deposit slips are there; they know that you've earned it, which they wouldn't know if you didn't put it in the bank.

Waitress: "That's true, I don't know."

My waitress is not unusual. Congress found that restaurant workers believe the possibility of an audit is so remote that they have become fearless.

Consider a waitress who, under the income tax, deprives the federal fisc of the revenue from the unreported tips at her marginal tax rate. Under a consumption tax, she might not only conceal the receipts but also claim a savings deduction for her deposits in her bank account. The consumption tax would thus provide a double benefit for underreporting by enabling individuals to consume a credible portion of their unreported receipts while deducting their savings from their reported receipts. This additional reward for noncompliance seems likely to increase incentives for nonreporting not only of tips but also of other common forms of unreported receipts (such as income from self-employment, moonlighting, dividends, interest, small businesses, and so forth). To the extent that a consumption tax requires borrowed amounts to be included in receipts, similar problems seem likely to emerge. One possible response of consumption tax proponents is that the deduction for savings will tend to stimulate reportable investments (opening savings accounts, for example, instead of hiding receipts in mattresses) and thereby facilitate IRS detection of underreporting. It nonetheless seems unlikely that our waitress, who has not been deterred under the income tax from depositing her unreported income in a savings account, would feel constrained from deducting these deposits on her consumption tax return.

Transactions involving capital gains currently account for a significant portion of unreported income from legal sources: about 11 percent of the total tax gap from individuals, according to an IRS estimate.[29] This estimate is consistent with Henry's claim that the overwhelming share of noncompliance with respect to legal source income appears to involve business and property income

29. *Tax Compliance Act of 1982*, p. 14.

and to involve upper-bracket taxpayers.[30] The stringent reporting requirements of the 1982 legislation do not seem likely to solve this underreporting problem, because noncompliance regarding estimated capital gains tends not to involve securities or commodities, but rather real estate, section 1231 exchanges, and collectibles such as coins, antiques, precious metals, and works of art.

The large share of total underreporting attributable to capital gain income provides a striking counterexample to the notion that lower rates will induce compliance. Sixty percent of income from capital gains is currently excluded from tax, and a top rate of 20 percent applies to capital gains in contrast to the maximum 50 percent rate that applies to ordinary income. A consumption tax would markedly increase the incentives for not reporting proceeds from the sale of capital assets, because all such proceeds could be included in receipts without either the exclusion for the taxpayer's "basis" or the 60 percent exclusion for the amount by which receipts exceed basis. The underreporting of receipts from the sale of property would therefore produce a greater loss of tax revenue under a consumption tax than under the present income tax, even ignoring the ability of taxpayers under a consumption tax to deduct as savings any reinvestment of their unreported receipts. This form of noncompliance would make the government a two-time loser under a consumption tax: the government not only would initially subsidize the purchase of the property by allowing its immediate deduction but would, upon sale of the property, fail either to recapture its initial investment or to collect tax on the investors' gain.

Finally, it is worth commenting briefly on the consumption tax problems of withholding. I, for one, do not regard it as accidental that the highest rates of compliance under the income tax, currently about 99 percent, involve wages from which taxes can effectively be withheld. In effect, income tax withholding makes involuntary the income tax reporting and collection process. Accurate withholding would almost certainly prove more difficult under an expenditure tax than under the current income tax. Withholding is currently estimated based on the taxpayer's wages adjusted for the average credits and deductions for that wage level. By contrast, under an expenditure tax, liability would turn not only on the taxpayer's wages but also on his or her expected allocation of income between consumption and savings. While

---

30. Henry, "Noncompliance with U.S. Tax Law."

wage withholding could probably be made as accurate in the aggregate under an expenditure tax as under the income tax, greater variations and withholding errors among individuals seem inevitable because of variations in saving for different individuals and for the same individual in different years. The greatest variations seem likely to be concentrated in the upper brackets, where Henry's data suggest that problems of income tax noncompliance are greatest. Moreover, as I have detailed elsewhere, increased information reporting, such as reporting of loans, would most likely be necessary under an expenditure tax.

In summary, it is certainly true that compliance is a serious problem under the current income tax. This problem demands attention, both at the level of theory and of fact, in order to design better compliance mechanisms and to improve those that already exist. The myopic notion that compliance problems would disappear, however, if we would but lower tax rates or shift from an income to a consumption tax does not withstand even this introductory analysis.

"Sickness comes in on horseback and goes out on foot":[31] *the problem of transition*

I have elsewhere considered general transitional problems of income tax reform and specifically considered transitional problems associated both with replacing income taxes by consumption taxes and with moving to a broad-based income tax.[32] All I can do here is to summarize the conclusion of that earlier work.

The 1982 minimum tax amendments should be regarded as an important first step toward a broad-based, lower-rate income tax. The new minimum tax has resolved such major obstacles as the treatment of capital gains, itemized deductions, and tax credits under a broad-based income tax and has partially resolved such other important issues as depletion and depreciation. Moreover, by using the minimum tax as the vehicle for transition, the difficult political task of setting broad-based income tax rates can be postponed, since the current minimum tax rate is within the range considered appropriate by flat-rate advocates.

Further base broadening is the necessary next step in the transition, and some important additions could be made to both the minimum tax and regular income tax bases. For example,

31. W. C. Hazlitt, *English Proverbs and Proverbial Phrases* (London: J. R. Smith, 1869), p. 366.

32. See Michael J. Graetz, "The 1982 Minimum Tax Amendments As a First Step in the Transition to a 'Flat-Rate' Tax," *University of Southern California Law Review*, vol. 56 (January 1983), pp. 527–71; and Graetz, "Implementing a Progressive Consumption Tax," pp. 1649–59.

Congress could expand the list of minimum tax preferences to include interest on state and local bonds and on life insurance reserves, unrealized gain on assets transferred by bequest and gift, the excess of allowable depreciation over economic depreciation, and the principal statutory exclusions from wages. It would still be necessary to resolve other difficult issues such as the taxation of fringe benefits. Indexing the tax base for inflation might also begin with the minimum tax.

Corporate tax revision could similarly be phased in if Congress decided to move toward a broad-based, low-rate income tax at both the individual and corporate levels. Again, the 1982 amendments may point the way by their 15 percent reduction of certain corporate tax preferences. Further reductions in such preferences could be enacted in conjunction with either a phaseout of the tax on corporate earnings distributed to shareholders as dividends or a general reduction of corporate tax rates. Alternatively, enactment of a new corporate "minimum tax on economic income" could serve as a transition vehicle to a broader-based corporate tax. Inflation adjustments and dividend relief (or denial of interest deductions) could be included in such a measure.

To move in the direction of consumption taxation, a value-added or retail sales tax could be phased in as the income tax was phased out. If Congress desired to apply a broad-based value-added or sales tax, while generally maintaining the current distribution of the tax burden, it should consider retaining an income tax for upper-income individuals. The current minimum tax, perhaps with further base-broadening amendments, could serve this function.

Only if an individualized, progressive tax on consumption were desired should Congress consider a so-called expenditure tax. The implementation of such a tax would raise a different set of transitional problems. For example, if a minimum tax on consumption were, as the Treasury Department has suggested, to serve as the transitional mechanism, the minimum tax of present law would first have to be restructured to apply to a consumption base.

Conclusion

The reports of the demise of the income tax, as of Mark Twain's death, are an exaggeration. To me, it seems no small irony that people such as William D. Andrews and John Chapoton, who favor replacing the income tax with a personal progressive tax on consumption—traditionally an "expenditure tax"—insist on calling such proposals a "cash flow income tax"[33] or a "consumed income tax."[34] These efforts to label consumption taxes as "income-type" taxes suggest to me a widespread recognition of the income tax as a symbol of tax justice. The income tax has come—rightly I believe—to embody the fundamental principle of justice that has guided U.S. tax policy throughout the twentieth century: that tax burdens should be distributed in accordance with people's ability to pay.

As Richard Musgrave put it, what is at stake is to "look for a general index of economic well-being which broadly measures a person's capacity to contribute or to 'sacrifice' on behalf of government. This is the tradition of taxation according to ability to pay."[35] Income is such a measure; wages or consumption alone are not. A tax system that relies solely on wages or consumption taxes fails to take into account ability to pay due to the accumulation of either capital or capital income. Moreover, if federal income taxation were to be replaced by consumption taxation in its most common form, as a retail sales or value-added tax, the tax burden of low- and middle-income citizens would increase relative to that of upper-income persons.

To explicitly reject the income tax in favor of a wage or consumption tax alone is therefore to reject this nation's commitment to taxation grounded on ability to pay. Proponents of such a change have failed so far to suggest am alternative criterion of justice in the distribution of tax burdens. Rather, they retain the income tax label to minimize the significance of the departure that they propose and to focus our attention on other criteria, most notably those of "economic efficiency" and "capital formation."

To exempt capital or capital income from tax (allegedly to promote economic efficiency and growth) conflicts directly with the goal of fair taxation tied to ability to pay; their exemption is neither permitted by the demands of tax equity nor compelled by evidence that such an exclusion is necessary for economic efficiency or economic growth. The challenge to tax policy in the years ahead is to achieve a modern reconciliation between the competing

33. Andrews, "A Consumption-Type or Cash Flow Personal Income Tax," pp. 113–19.

34. See, for example, "Treasury Fact Sheet on Tax Reform," *Tax Notes*, vol. 22 (February 6, 1984), p. 444.

35. Richard A. Musgrave, "In Defense of an Income Concept," *Harvard Law Review*, vol. 81 (November 1967), pp. 44, 45–46.

claims of equity and economic efficiency. Surely it is possible to achieve income taxation that distorts saving and investment far less than the present regime and still to impose a rate of taxation on capital or capital income that exceeds zero, the consumption tax rate. The income tax needs restructuring, not repeal. For as Joe E. Brown said to Tony Curtis in *Some Like It Hot,* after learning to his great dismay that Curtis was a man pretending to be a woman: "Well, nobody's perfect."

Comment by John S. Nolan

I AGREE with Michael Graetz that the income tax should continue to be our major source of revenue because it is fundamentally fairer taxation based on the principle of ability to pay. I agree also that the income tax base can be restored, although it will be done only gradually and incrementally and not in any single broad stroke such as the Bradley-Gephardt plan in its present form. I agree also that a personal, progressive expenditure tax offers no advantage over gradual restoration of our income tax structure; it would be levied on an inherently narrower base and it presents the same political and compliance problems that we face in restoring our income tax structure. I particularly agree that restoration requires that we deal with the problems of inflation and double taxation of corporate earnings which have been root causes of the disintegration of the income tax base over the last twenty-five years. My disagreement with Graetz is that these conclusions provide no adequate solution to our structural deficits problem, and I suggest that they call for introduction of a value-added tax while we put in place a long-term, gradual plan for rebuilding our income tax system.

Expenditure tax problems

Dealing first with proposals for a personal, progressive expenditure tax, Graetz quite correctly points out that we would still have to solve the treatment of fringe benefits, home mortgage and consumer interest, charitable contributions, the taxation of government transfer payments, and many of the other major gaps in our existing income tax base. It is equally wrong to assume that issues such as the existing preferences for state and local bonds or real estate investment or others would go away; the powerful lobbies seeking a preference for such investments would continue to do so, and there are convenient ways to achieve a negative tax rate in an expenditure tax framework. The compliance problem of unreported receipts would continue to exist and might even be magnified as a deduction for investments was granted.

Even more fundamentally, however, I suggest that our political process would not tolerate a tax system that permitted without restraint by taxation the growth of larger and larger fortunes. The unexercised consumptive capacity of the very wealthy would go untaxed even though they would have all the power and influence that comes with wealth. Of course, we have much of that condition today under our existing, decimated income tax structure, but I think our fundamental long-term goal should continue to be a rebuilding of that income tax structure, not an endorsement of tax avoidance.

What this suggests is that a personal expenditure tax would at best be an addition to our existing, unsatisfactory income tax system. Treasury has considered using an expenditure tax as a more rational form of minimum tax; it would in all events tax income consumed, even though such income might escape the basic income tax structure because of tax shelter opportunities. The added complexity would, however, be intolerable. As Graetz suggests, we already have in place an individual alternative minimum tax that, if all else fails, can be gradually expanded to restore the tax base. That is a far better direction in which to go.

There are other fundamental problems in moving to an expenditure tax, not the least of which is a constitutional one. Borrowed funds should be part of the tax base, but can we tax borrowed funds under the Sixteenth Amendment when they are not reinvested? The transitional problems, as Graetz suggests, are horrendous. What do we do about the existing investments of individuals which have been purchased out of after-tax dollars? Can we fairly tax persons upon liquidating these previously acquired investments if they do not reinvest?

Bradley-Gephardt problems

Instead, I would propose that we recognize 1985 for what it will be—a golden opportunity to put in place a long-term plan for gradually restoring the income tax while at the same time remedying its fundamental defects. Bradley-Gephardt seeks to go too far too fast in several major respects and does nothing to solve the fundamental defects in our present income tax structure arising out of inflation and double taxation of corporate earnings; in fact it exacerbates them. It cuts the existing, meaningful limits on qualified retirement plans in half and eliminates cost-of-living adjustments in the dollar limits. The result will be gradually to phase out those benefits and the beneficial averaging effects they bring to our income tax system. Bradley-Gephardt in effect limits the benefits of charitable contributions, the home mortgage interest deduction, state and local income and real estate tax deductions, and the individual retirement account deduction to a 14 percent credit by making these amounts deductible only against income taxed at the 14 percent rate. Bradley-Gephardt increases the capital gain rate from 20 percent to 30 percent in most cases without introducing any inflation adjustment.

Long-term solutions

Next year will be a golden year because of the growing congressional and public recognition of the need for a stronger and simpler income tax system. The first year of any new administration is the best year politically to put in place a major tax reform— witness the year 1969. Rather than take on all the same old major political battles that the Bradley-Gephardt type of plan would recreate, we should persuade Congress to adopt a long-term strategy. As to individuals, Congress should provide for gradual expansion of the alternative minimum tax structure, which currently adds a long list of tax preferences to adjusted gross income and limits personal deductions to charitable contributions, extraordinary medical deductions and casualty losses, interest on mortgage loans, and other interest expense. Further, these interest deductions are limited to the amount of the taxpayer's investment income. The taxpayer must pay a tax of 20 percent of this expanded income tax base. The list of preferences could be substantially expanded in gradual increments to include statutory fringe benefits and various shelter benefits not now included. The rate structure could be expanded to decrease the $40,000 joint-return threshold and build in several rates to achieve some progressivity. The interest deduction could be further restricted to the mortgage on the principal residence.

The same process could be extended to corporations. The existing cut-back in specified preferences by 15 percent (20 percent in the current Senate bill) could be enlarged each year for five years by 5 percent per year, and the list of preferences could be gradually expanded.

At the same time, however, it is fundamentally important to begin gradually also to build into the system basis adjustments for inflation and mitigation of the double taxation of distributed corporate earnings. A shareholder credit can be appropriately limited to corporate tax actually paid with respect to the portion of corporate earnings that is distributed. We must recognize that making arbitrary responses, such as increasing the investment credit and introducing accelerated cost recovery, instead of indexing the basis of assets, has led to the ever-expanding tax shelter industry that has been a principal cause of the narrowing of our tax base. This may indeed be a central cause of our increasing noncompliance problem as a large number of taxpayers, unable to use legal tax shelters because of the need for cash, fashion their own nonlegal shelters. I am not as certain as Graetz about the need to deal with the debt side of the equation, but I see every reason to expand limitations of the interest deduction at both the individual and corporate levels. We have attempted this for individuals, so far ineffectively, by limiting the investment interest deduction in section 163(d) and more recently and more effectively, as I have suggested, in the alternative minimum tax changes introduced for individuals in 1982.

Similarly, it is fundamentally important to address our inherent structural problem of double taxation of distributed corporate earnings. All too often this furnishes the rationale for continuation or expansion of tax preferences even though this rationale is largely a misconception. Substantial amounts of retained corporate earnings enjoy these preferences and are never taxed to shareholders because of the capital gains exclusion or the exclusion of appreciation at death. With an appropriate corporate income tax, we can much more rationally reconsider the need for existing corporate tax preferences. Such a tax would reduce the skewing of the existing system toward debt financing and away from equity financing.

The foregoing proposals will do nothing to simplify the existing income tax structure. They may actually add to its complexity. Introduction of a broadly based, low-rate value-added tax to deal with the structural deficits problem while we gradually repair the income tax base will surely add to the complexity of the tax structure as a whole. But this is complexity we can accept, because it largely affects only business and high-income taxpayers, who can readily cope with it. It is much more important to rebuild the existing foundation of our federal tax structure, the income tax, because it is the fairest system for allocating the tax burden.

It is the gradual disintegration of this fairness in allocation of the burden that has led to our most serious problem—widespread noncompliance. This problem will continue to exist in any form of cash flow or expenditure tax if it is perceived as unfair, as I think it would be. The noncompliance problem results from the widespread perception that a relative minority is able to take advantage of tax shelters and other publicized tax avoidances.

Persons not able to take advantage of these measures fashion their own tax shelters by noncompliance. We must rebuild our tax structure on a basis that is perceived as being fair to everyone. A system that allows an unlimited deduction for savings will not be so perceived.

Summary

The problem of rebuilding the income tax structure is one of transition—dealing with the existing, entrenched interests reflected in the almost endless number of current tax expenditures. These expenditures must be phased out gradually and incrementally over a period of at least five to ten years in a slow process, such as by expansion of the alternative minimum tax concept and gradual disallowance of corporate tax preferences. Revenue needs in the interim can be funded by a value-added tax constructed so as to be nonregressive by providing a refundable income tax credit to lower-income taxpayers. If levied on a very broad base at fairly low rates, it will be reasonably simple to administer and no less fair than our existing income tax structure, which is progressive only in name. Such a value-added tax will not present serious compliance problems and will give us the time we need to restore the income tax system to its proper place. The goal should be to obtain a congressional commitment to rebuild the income tax over a period of years into a reasonably progressive tax on a much broader base, at lower rates, with appropriate adjustments to provide for inflation and eliminate or at least greatly moderate the double taxation of corporate earnings.

Comment by Emil M. Sunley

I AM VERY PLEASED to have this opportunity to say nice things about Michael Graetz's paper. I believe I was chosen for this assignment because for a number of years I was one of the few economists under the age of forty who believed in the income tax. Unfortunately this is no longer true, but it is not because I have changed my view of the income tax.

In addressing his subject of whether the income tax can continue to be a principal revenue source, Graetz touches on all the major issues: tax expenditures, inflation, depreciation or capital recovery, integration of the corporate and individual income taxes, tax compliance, and transition problems to a new tax. I will comment briefly on some of these issues.

Tax expenditures may be a lingering problem of the 1960s, but important lessons have been learned from the battles waged since the first tax expenditure budget was published in 1968; the most important of these is that in the political arena there are very few tax purists. The argument that a particular tax expenditure is bad tax policy carries little weight. The many exclusions, deductions, and credits that have been added to the tax law as special preferences must each be evaluated using the same criteria that are used for evaluating direct government expenditures. These criteria include whether and how much government aid is needed and whether the tax system is the most efficient mechanism for delivering that aid.

The debate over broadly based, low-rate income taxes also has been instructive. When Congress must raise revenue to reduce the federal deficit, it should give priority to base broadening—that is, to removing tax preferences no longer needed or of lower priority. Similarly, when Congress must reduce spending to reduce the federal deficit, it should reduce or eliminate those spending programs no longer needed or of lower priority.

Graetz clearly identifies the three major problems with an income tax: inflation, depreciation or capital recovery, and the integration of the individual and corporate taxes. But Graetz does not jump to the conclusion that we should solve these problems by going to a broad-based consumption tax. Instead he recognizes that the practical choice is not between a broad-based income tax and a broad-based consumption tax. If income is chosen as the appropriate measure of the ability to pay, there will continue to be significant departures from the ideal tax base. If consumption is chosen, there will also be significant departures from this ideal tax base. The realistic choice is between an income tax that excludes major portions of income such as unrealized gains and losses and a consumption tax that excludes major types of consumption, such as housing and food.

My one major criticism of the Graetz paper is that it does not address the issue of whether the revenue yield of the income tax and other federal revenue sources can be increased sufficiently to reduce the federal deficit significantly. Though I believe the income tax will continue to be a major revenue source, the issue that the nation, the administration, and the Congress must face is whether the income tax must be supplemented with an entirely new federal tax, most likely the value-added tax. On this issue reasonable people can and do differ.

Arguments for a major new revenue source

The gap between federal spending and revenues is now running at more than 5 percent of gross national product. Practically no one believes that a gap of that magnitude can be closed by reducing spending alone, particularly given projected increases in defense spending. If it is assumed that the gap is closed half by reducing spending and half by increasing taxes, taxes would have to increase by 2.5 percent of GNP. Given that income taxes are now equal to 10 percent of GNP, income taxes would have to rise by 25 percent—equivalent to a 25 percent surcharge. To accomplish this by base broadening would be a Herculean task equivalent to cleaning the Augean stables.

The Tax Equity and Fiscal Responsibility Act of 1982 may give some comfort to those who believe base broadening can restore federal revenues. This legislation was enacted in response to concerns that the Economic Recovery Tax Act of 1981 went too far in reducing taxes. Though the 1982 bill let stand the scheduled individual tax reductions enacted in 1981, it significantly cut back the cornerstone of the business portion of the 1981 act, the accelerated cost recovery system. In addition, it reduced certain corporate preferences by 15 percent, imposed restrictions on tax leasing, tightened taxation of foreign oil and gas income, and reduced the tax benefits from investing in Puerto Rico. A key reform element of the 1982 legislation was imposition of withholding on interest and dividends. Over all, the 1982 law is expected to increase fiscal 1987 receipts by $61 billion, equal to 1.3 percent of GNP.

Though some would view the 1982 act as a "good start" in closing the deficit gap through income tax base broadening, the events of 1983 and 1984 give less comfort. In 1983 Congress passed a budget resolution instructing the tax-writing committees to raise $73 billion of additional revenue in the fiscal 1984–86 period, but the first session of the 98th Congress adjourned with the requirements of the resolution ignored and forgotten. Moreover, Congress in 1983 repealed withholding on interest and dividends before it went into effect.

It now appears likely that Congress in 1984 will enact a tax increase in the range of $50 billion over the fiscal 1984–87 period. This "down payment" on the deficit, though politically and psychologically significant, is very modest. If one takes the House-passed version of this legislation, 70 percent of the revenue comes from deferring or repealing tax reductions scheduled to go into effect in 1984 or later, limiting leasing to tax-exempt entities, and reducing the benefits from income averaging. This year's legislation will have only a very small impact on the deficits projected by the president. He proposed $14 billion of increased revenues in his budget for fiscal year 1987; the House bill would increase revenues by $21 billion. The difference is only a $7 billion reduction in the president's projected deficit of $180 billion in fiscal year 1987. That is not much for a 1,000-page tax bill.

Arguments against a major new revenue source

Though the federal deficit should be reduced, it is not clear that it needs to be eliminated over the next several years. An interim goal might be to reduce the federal deficit to about 1 percent of GNP by reducing spending by 2 percent of GNP and increasing revenues by 2 percent of GNP. Is this an impossible task? Over the last three years Congress has reduced federal revenues by more than 2 percent of GNP, from a high of 20.8 percent of GNP in fiscal 1981 to 18.6 percent of GNP this year. All that is necessary now is to increase revenues by 2 percent of GNP.

But it is not necessary to go back to where we were in 1981. Instead, we could go back to 1974, before Congress enacted the Tax Reduction Act of 1975, the Tax Reform Act of 1976, the Tax Reduction and Simplification Act of 1977, the Revenue Act of 1978, the Economic Recovery Tax Act of 1981, and the Tax Equity and Fiscal Responsibility Act of 1982. At that time federal taxes were 19.1 percent of GNP, compared with 18.6 percent in 1984. The major difference between 1974 and 1984 is the sharp increase in social insurance taxes from 5.4 to 6.7 percent of GNP. Federal revenues, excluding social insurance taxes, were 13.7 percent of GNP in 1974, almost 2 percentage points higher than the 11.9 percent share for the same taxes in 1984. Federal revenues can be increased by almost 2 percent of GNP by simply restoring income taxes, estate and gift taxes, excise taxes, and other receipts to their 1974 levels as a share of GNP.

One way to increase federal revenues by 2 percent of GNP would be to increase income taxes by 1.3 percent of GNP, estate and gift taxes by 0.1 percent of GNP, and excise taxes and other receipts by 0.6 percent of GNP. These increases would enlarge federal revenue by $92 billion in fiscal 1987. If income taxes were increased by 1.3 percent of GNP they would be slightly higher than they were in fiscal 1974 but significantly below what they were in 1980 or 1981. An increase of 0.1 percent of GNP in estate and gift taxes would restore these taxes to their 1980 level. The 0.6 percent of GNP increase in excise taxes and other receipts would restore these taxes and receipts to their 1974 level after one takes into account the small increase in excise taxes contained in this year's tax legislation.

Unfortunately, as a discussant I have been given only twenty minutes today, and therefore there is not time for me to reveal the full details of my tax program. But let me assure you I have a plan for ending the war, and if elected I will restore equity, efficiency, and simplicity to our tax system. I can say, however, my plan would involve going after some sacred cows such as the deductibility of consumer interest—a proposal that should be endorsed by those who favor a consumption tax. I would want to take a hard look at the depreciation of real estate and possible limitations on the amount of artificial tax deductions that can be used to offset unrelated income—the latter, a proposal endorsed by Graetz. If sufficient revenue from the income tax cannot be raised by reducing or repealing special exclusions, deductions, and credits, as a last resort I would support a 5 percent surcharge, which was President Reagan's contingency tax proposal in 1983. Such a surcharge, applying to corporations and individuals, would increase federal revenue by almost $24 billion in fiscal 1987. Many will argue that income tax changes of the type I am describing are politically unrealistic. This may be true. But the political consensus two years ago was that Congress would never tax social security benefits.

Before anyone buys my secret plan for raising taxes, maybe I should reveal the alternative—a value-added tax. Let me suggest, without supporting evidence, that it is probably not worthwhile to impose such a tax to raise revenue equal to only 2 percent of GNP. The more likely scenario is a value-added tax with a 10 percent rate. Given the usual exemptions and exceptions, this tax would increase revenues by about 3.4 percent of GNP,[1] providing the additional revenue that would be needed to buy off the states, redress its own regressivity problems, reduce corporate or individual income taxes, and finance increased federal spending. Before one signs on to a value-added tax, one will want to have some understanding of just how the additional revenues will be used. In fact, this is the crucial question to be answered before endorsing a major new weapon for the government's tax arsenal.

1. Personal consumption expenditures are about 65 percent of GNP. With exemptions for direct and imputed rents, medical care and drugs, private education, charitable activities, and state and local governments, the base of a value-added tax might equal 45 percent of GNP. The gross revenue yield of a 10 percent value-added tax would then be 4.5 percent of GNP. The value-added tax, however, would reduce the base for the income tax: someone's income, as a share of GNP, must be lower if indirect business taxes have gone up. Assuming that the marginal income tax rate on an additional dollar of GNP is 25 percent, the net result of a 10 percent value-added tax would be increased revenues of 3.4 percent.

The Bradley-Gephardt Fair Tax

RICHARD A. GEPHARDT

Now THAT the president has said that we'll have tax reform if he's reelected, and all the Democratic candidates have endorsed the idea of tax reform, I suppose we can expect an intensified debate next year, if not actual action, on far-reaching reform of the Internal Revenue Code. At the end of my remarks, however, I will bring us back to earth and remind us how difficult the legislative process actually is, even if the president, whoever he is, supports tax reform and even if there is substantial support for it in the Congress.

Background

Let me try to explain the thinking behind the Bradley-Gephardt Fair Tax Act (S.1421) and then briefly run through its major provisions. Two or three years ago I began looking at how we could reform the tax code. I started out thinking that a consumption-based tax would be the best. After going up and down that mountain three or four times looking at what the end result would be and how difficult it would be to get there, I came to the conclusion that a consumption tax wasn't the best way to go. At that point I became more interested in how we could bring about tax reform within the context of the present system. In that process I became aware that Senator Bill Bradley was doing the same thing, and so we began to work together on the Bradley-Gephardt bill. I've been on the Ways and Means Committee for seven and a half years now. I've gone through three or four major bills and a number of not-so-major bills. Having lived through that exercise again and again, I came to the conclusion that it was time to talk about basic tax reform. We have so riddled the code with preferences, exceptions, and deductions, that the tax system doesn't make economic sense or tax sense anymore. Through the years the code has become a system that makes citizens distrust one another and their government. When that point is reached, you have to begin to examine whether or not you've got the kind of system you want.

74

Provisions   So Bill Bradley and I came up with our version of substantial tax reform. The Bradley-Gephardt Fair Tax Act is a variation on the flat-tax theme. It deals with broadening the tax base and lowering the rate. The rates we came up with are 14 percent on individual income up to $25,000 or joint income up to $40,000; 26 percent on individual income between $25,000 and $37,500 or joint income between $40,000 and $65,000; and 30 percent on individual income exceeding $37,500 or joint income in excess of $65,000. It has been estimated that more than 70 percent of taxpayers would pay at the 14 percent rate.

As to personal exemptions, we propose a $1,600 exemption per person on individual and joint returns, $1,800 for a head of household, and $1,000 for dependents; thus a husband and wife with two children would get a personal exemption of $5,200.

The standard deduction for those who do not itemize would be increased to $3,000 for individual returns and $6,000 for joint returns. Thus, through a combination of the $6,000 standard deduction and the $5,200 personal exemptions, a family of four could earn up to $11,200 before being subject to tax.

We do retain some deductions, believing that politically we really cannot achieve substantial reform unless some of the most popular and some of the most used deductions are kept. But our deductions can only be taken against the 14 percent basic rate. Each dollar spent on a deductible expense would yield a tax reduction of only 14 cents. Retained deductions include home mortgage interest; state and local income and real property taxes; charitable deductions; medical expenses exceeding 10 percent of income; and IRA and Keogh contributions.

Obviously, we have eliminated many deductions and preferences, such as the deduction for two-earner couples; the preferential capital gains rate; income averaging; indexing; and the interest and dividend exclusions. The list of eliminated deductions is long, and I'm sure that some of your favorites are on the list. But I urge you, as you consider this plan, not just to fix on what's eliminated, but also to look at the lower rate, which is the trade-off in this kind of tax system.

On the corporate side the bill establishes a flat 30 percent rate on corporate income. A new, class-life depreciation plan simplifies the existing system while keying depreciation periods more closely to actual asset life. It's a depreciation system that's not as liberal as the one we have in place today but is simpler, fairer, and still allows an adequate depreciation allowance.

*Revenue
impact*

The revenue impact of the Bradley-Gephardt bill would be the same as that of the present law, provided that neither system incorporates indexing. If you compare our plan with the present tax structure including indexation, we pick up many billions of dollars over the next ten years. If you assume our plan were indexed, the revenue impact would be exactly the same as the present law's.

We tried hard not to confuse this debate over tax reform with the debate over how much revenue the government should raise or how much should come from corporations. If we attempt to reform the income taxes, those questions will and should be debated. But we would like to keep everyone's eye on tax reform and not get it confused with other fundamental tax issues. I have no doubt that developing and enacting a tax reform proposal will be politically difficult. We have seen how Congress has labored over tax bills in the past few years. When one contemplates all the deductions and preferences that are now in the tax code and that we propose to exclude, one gets some measure of the practical difficulty of full comprehensive reform.

But I also believe that 1985 may be the year that this could happen. We face large and growing deficits. There is an interest in basic budgetary reform, both on the spending and the revenue side; and it may be that some combination of deficit reductions could be put together that would include basic tax reform. With support from the general public, something like our plan could be adopted over the objection of the lobbies that do not want their particular gimmick touched. I don't know the odds facing the Fair Tax bill, but I do believe that it has a chance and probably a better chance than it had three, or five, or ten years ago, when tax reform was pretty well laughed off the stage.

*Support
for reform*

Political support for tax reform in the country now is very high. You can argue that many people don't fully understand either the problems or the proposed solutions. Certainly this is true in many cases. But I think a growing number of people in the corporate world and among individual taxpayers are really disturbed and put off by the present tax system. If a full measure of that feeling can be transmitted to Washington, tax reform may become a reality.

Obviously there are those who support competitors to the Fair Tax Act. Some support the consumption tax; others favor a totally flat tax; still others propose the addition of selective excise taxes or general sales or value-added taxes to the present system. There are numerous variations on these themes. I'm sure many will be aired this year and next. I look forward to the debate that's to come as we really get down to brass tacks and see if some tax reform can be achieved.

I believe tax reform would be good for the economy; it would be good for tax policy; and it would be good for the taxpayer. People's faith and confidence in our tax system has been eroded to a dangerous point, and we should restore some of that faith with basic tax reform.

Alternatives to the Income Tax

GORDON D. HENDERSON

WHAT DISTINGUISHES this meeting on tax reform from so many others in the past is that we must now find a way to eliminate large federal deficits, and we must do so at a time when public discontent with the present tax system has never been higher; when voters' hopes have been fanned by political oratory promising new tax systems that will be wondrously simple and will have lower rates; and when economists seem to have reached growing agreement that we should tilt our tax system away from the income tax toward a consumption tax.

Grounds for complaint about the present tax structure

Before we can evaluate new forms of tax that might substitute for or supplement our present tax structure, we need to examine the dissatisfaction with the present structure. Only then can we assess the extent to which the new forms may provide a solution to these problems as well as to the deficit problem. The most frequently voiced complaints are these:

Complexity

The federal income tax has grown too complex for taxpayers to understand or for the Internal Revenue Service to administer efficiently. Complexity is not an inherent characteristic of the income tax, however. In its early stages the income tax was quite simple. The problem lies in our political structure and particularly in the structure of Congress. The changes that have taken place in the organization of Congress in the last two decades have weakened the discipline formerly exerted by the parties and by committee chairmen. A fragmented, every-member-for-himself Congress is unable to resist the temptation to use the tax law to give something to every pressure group (even tax reformers get a share) and to try to solve every national problem with a tax incentive or tax burden. The problem is accelerating. Each success by a pressure group simply ensures that all groups will redouble their efforts.

The main appeal of many of the new tax systems being proposed

78

lies in their presumed simplicity. But it is unlikely that Congress will adopt anything simple, and if it does, it is certain it will not let it stay that way for long. We should be cautious, therefore, about trying to work a revolutionary rather than an evolutionary change in tax structure when the cost of a revolutionary change is a certain and immediate upset in expectations and when the desired benefit is so unlikely to be achieved. The real solution to the complexity problem lies in a change in the way Congress addresses tax legislation, and unfortunately no such change is in sight.

Noncompliance

The press tells us the American people believe that they or their neighbors cut corners in one way or another on their income tax, that taxpayer morality is on the decline, and that the voluntary nature of our self-assessment system is eroding. The causes for this are complex, and they do not all relate to taxes. Taxes are not the only area where compliance does not seem to be what it used to be. The delinquency rate on government student loans, for example, is an astonishing 13 percent (the defaulters include 270 Harvard medical school graduates).[1] But surely one of the more important contributors to tax noncompliance (and perhaps to most other forms of noncompliance as well) has been inadequate enforcement. The Internal Revenue Service has not been given a large enough audit force. Everyone is aware that the percentage of returns audited has been declining. One gets the idea that Congress doesn't believe enough in the tax law it has created to want to see it enforced properly. The combination of a complex law (and one the public doesn't think is very fair) with an inadequate audit force makes the "audit lottery" a significant factor in actual experience, and so the problem feeds upon itself. The most important thing that could be done to improve compliance is to expand the number of auditors.

The Individual's Tax Burden

The proportion of federal tax collections represented by corporate taxes has been declining, whereas the proportion coming from individuals has been growing. The same thing has been happening with state-level collections. The cause lies in rising government expenditures and inflation combined with the graduated nature of the personal income tax (one of the few graduated-

---

1. *Tax Notes*, vol. 20 (September 12, 1983), p. 895.

rate taxes we have). Inflation, rising employment taxes, and bracket creep in the income tax have caused the marginal federal tax rate for the median income family of four persons to rise from 22 percent in 1975 to 24 percent in 1981 and to a projected 32 percent by 1985, an increase of 34 percent in ten years.[2]

Because the corporate tax is essentially a flat tax, there has been little bracket creep in the corporate sector. Moreover, recent tax changes mainly applicable to corporations, such as the combination of the investment tax credit with accelerated cost recovery, have helped reduce the impact of inflation on capital investment by corporations.

Individuals, on the other hand, are well aware of the twin scourges of a progressive income tax and inflation, and although inflation rates are now much diminished from recent levels, they are still high. The staff of the Joint Committee on Taxation, in an excellent 1977 report on capital formation, pointed out that although the federal government could not constitutionally adopt a wealth tax (because the Constitution forbids imposition of direct taxes by the federal government unless the proceeds are apportioned among the states on the basis of population), the net effect of the present income tax combined with inflation is to impose a wealth tax each year, which is generally equal to the rate of inflation times the marginal income tax rate.[3] In short, a 6 percent inflation rate combined with a 50 percent marginal tax rate represents an annual wealth tax of 3 percent. Combined with a 20 percent marginal rate it represents an annual wealth tax of 1.2 percent.

At the same time, the public's romance with "soak-the-rich" marginal rates has been souring a bit in recent years as more and more American families have been pushed into higher brackets. Listen, for example, to what a Harvard Law School professor, of all people, wrote in the *New York Times* as far back as 1976: "I suspect that a large number of Americans . . . believe that it is demoralizing for *everybody* when millions of hard-working people are embittered and their initiative is sapped by the thought that more than half of every extra dollar they work for will go to Federal, state and local governments."[4] Moreover, although the

2. Mark O. Hatfield, "Tax Reform: It's Time to Fulfill the Promise," *Tax Notes*, vol. 22 (January 30, 1984), pp. 407, 411 (quoting testimony of David Stockman).

3. Joint Committee on Taxation, *Tax Policy and Capital Formation*, Committee Print, prepared for the Task Force on Capital Formation of the House Ways and Means Committee, 94 Cong. 2 sess. (Government Printing Office, 1977), p. 26.

4. Charles Fried, "Carter's Tax Program," *New York Times*, October 18, 1976.

politicians have tried hard not to let the people in on the secret, the fact is that there is not enough money in the hands of the "rich" to support the expanded claims of government. Even confiscation of taxable incomes greater than $50,000 would run the federal government for only about three weeks, whereas the deficit represents almost three months of federal expenditures.

In short, despite the public's dissatisfaction with the tax burden that has been imposed on individuals, the fact is that the broad middle class is going to have to bear the brunt of higher (not lower) taxes unless the American people are willing to vote for sharp reductions in expenditures for social security, medicare, and defense. This will be true even if the corporate tax is raised. The only questions, really, are the form in which these taxes are to be imposed and the extent to which inflation will be added to the mix.

Economic Distortions

Everyone, whether enamoured of the income tax or not, seems to agree that our present income tax discourages savings. There has also been growing concern by people of all political persuasions that Americans have been saving less than citizens of other developed countries, which is thought to translate into less-than-adequate capital investment in the American economy and, in the end, lower economic growth rates.

Theoreticians divide taxes into accretion and consumption taxes. Accretion taxes, of which income taxes are an example, tax the sum of personal consumption plus accumulation. Consumption taxes are imposed only on consumption. Accretion taxes make saving difficult because money received is taxed before it can be saved, and then the earnings on the savings themselves are taxed again. When inflation is combined with an accretion tax, the adverse impact on savings is magnified. Without the indexing both of rates and of historical cost figures, inflation artificially enlarges taxable income from capital (except for taxpayers heavily in debt).

The 1977 Joint Committee study on capital formation pointed out that our present tax system, by combining inflation and an accretion tax without indexing, in substance imposes both an accretion tax and a wealth tax. Together these two elements form a deadly attack on saving rates and capital formation.

William D. Andrews has pointed out that our present accretion type of income tax contains departures from the accretion tax ideal that discriminate in favor of people who are already wealthy and against people who have to earn their wealth before they can accumulate it.[5] This is because a pure accretion tax would tax not only cash receipts but all increases in wealth each year, whether realized or unrealized. But such a pure accretion tax is impracticable. It would require annual valuations of all property, and it would require taxes to be paid in cash even when all that has occurred is a growth in the value of property owned by the taxpayer, such as farms or homes or securities. The inability to tax changes in unrealized values distorts the way that an actual accretion tax treats the accumulation portion of its tax base. Money saved out of ordinary income and invested in a way that produces currently taxable earnings, such as the typical savings account funded out of salary, is taxed in both respects; accretions of wealth through unrealized appreciation of existing assets are not taxed currently and, under our present system, are even taxed at a low rate when realized.

To achieve a perfect accretion tax, we would have to eliminate deferral and also the low rate for capital gains. As Andrews points out, our failure to do so allows the already wealthy to get wealthier and ultimately to pay a lower tax, and it discriminates against those without present wealth who need to save for retirement and emergencies, which for most people are the main reasons for saving. Our present tax structure even adds to the deferral aspect by allowing for tax-free reorganizations, tax-free exchanges of realty, and installment treatment of sales.

Aside from the adverse impact on saving, our tax structure creates other economic distortions. One of these is the double layer of tax created by the corporate tax. Because of the double tax, investments in most corporate equities are not attractive except for the potential for capital gain appreciation. This, in addition to influencing the allocation of capital investment, may also have a subtle distortive effect on corporate behavior. It places a premium on the market activity of stock rather than on long-term earnings and yields. The resulting emphasis on short-term earnings per share may increase the tendency of American management to adopt a short-term rather than a long-term outlook. Moreover, the fact that interest on debt is deductible by corpo-

5. William D. Andrews, "A Consumption-Type or Cash Flow Personal Income Tax," *Harvard Law Review*, vol. 87 (April 1974), pp. 1113–19. See also Alvin C. Warren, Jr., "Fairness and a Consumption-Type or Cash-Flow Personal Income Tax," *Harvard Law Review*, vol. 88 (March 1975), pp. 931–45; William D. Andrews, "Fairness and the Personal Income Tax: A Reply to Professor Warren," *Harvard Law Review*, vol. 88 (March 1975), pp. 947–58; Michael J. Graetz, "Implementing a Progressive Consumption Tax," *Harvard Law Review*, vol. 92 (June 1979), p. 1595.

rations but dividend payments to shareholders are not encourages corporations to become more highly leveraged than is healthy.

Investment decisions have in general been distorted by special tax advantages granted to particuar forms of investment. It is no accident that the lists of the wealthiest Americans published recently by *Forbes* magazine contain a disproportionate number of persons who have made their money in real estate or oil.[6] Both of these activities enjoy special tax advantages. In fact, for a good many years now, it might be said that it has not really paid Americans to save unless they could invest their funds in some type of tax-benefited investment, whether it is one that will produce immediate deductions, such as individual retirement accounts or pension plans, or capital gains, or both, such as oil and gas or real estate investments. We should work toward eliminating the distortive effects of the tax structure.

Yet, with respect to capital formation, we should not expect too much from a tax system. Even a favorable tax system will not result in adequate capital investment or economic growth unless other conditions for favorable economic activity are there in abundance, such as a stable currency and a favorable and not too rapidly changing political and regulatory climate.

Alternatives or substitutes for the present income tax

Proposed substitutes for our present income tax take two different approaches. One approach would try to simplify and strengthen the income tax through proposals for a broad-based flat tax or compressed-rate tax, which are all sometimes referred to as "comprehensive income" taxes. These proposals would take away the special provisions and incentives of the present income tax, reduce the number of rate brackets, and lower the rates. The second group of proposals would replace our income tax with a cash flow consumption tax.

The essential difference between these two approaches lies in their impact on saving. The comprehensive income taxes would worsen the current distortion in saving, whereas the cash flow consumption tax would offer individuals greater encouragement than they now have to save.

Comprehensive Income: The Flat Tax

Concerned with the complexity and eroding tax base of our present income tax, some have proposed that we substitute for it

6. "The Forbes Four Hundred," *Forbes* (Fall 1983), p. 71.

a new, "flat" tax. This tax would disallow almost all exclusions from income and almost all deductions now available to individuals except business deductions. To such an expanded tax base would be applied a single rate of tax. John Chapoton, assistant secretary of the treasury for tax policy, testified in 1982 that a broad-based flat tax of 16 percent that allowed a $2,000 personal exemption ($3,000 per joint return) could raise the same revenue as the then-current income tax.[7] It is instructive to note, however, that he also testified that a cash flow consumption tax (broad-based tax that allowed deductions for savings) could do the same thing with a rate of only 17 percent, a number that leaves me skeptical, because it assumes that savings will not increase under such a tax. He also said that our present individual income tax base could raise the same revenue with a single rate of 19 percent.

However, a single-rate tax would greatly increase the relative burden on the lower-income portion of the taxpaying spectrum while reducing it for the wealthy. In my judgment this is simply not politically desirable or feasible. Because of this discrimination against lower-income taxpayers, the flat-rate idea has evolved into proposals that retain the base-broadening concept but couple it with a graduated rate schedule, though one that has fewer and lower rates than our present system.

Comprehensive Income: Broad-Based, Compressed-Rate Taxes

The Treasury Department's 1977 *Blueprints for Basic Tax Reform* contained a detailed proposal for a broadened tax base to which would be applied a graduated rate scale containing fewer and lower rates than the present tax.[8] It would broaden the base by including in income social security benefits, employment taxes paid by employers for medicare, employer-paid premiums for life and health insurance, the growth in cash value of permanent life insurance policies, unemployment compensation, all cash transfer payments from government (including veterans' disability and survivors' benefits, veterans' pensions, aid to families with dependent children, supplemental security income, workers' compensation, and a portion of the value of food stamps), 100 percent of capital gains (but with a basis adjustment for inflation), and tax-exempt bond interest. (Note that such a proposal would presumably broaden the base for employment taxes as well as for income taxes.)

7. Bureau of National Affairs, *Daily Tax Report,* no. 188 (September 28, 1982), pp. J-10–J-11.

8. U.S. Department of the Treasury, *Blueprints for Basic Tax Reform* (GPO, 1977).

The *Blueprints* proposal would deny deductions (except those related to business) for all state and local property taxes, state and local sales taxes, medical expenses, charitable contributions, and casualty losses. It would continue to allow deductions for state and local income taxes and for interest payments (including those on home mortgages and consumer loans). All earnings on pension funds would be taxed. The corporate tax would be eliminated, and shareholders of all corporations would be taxed as if the corporation were a subchapter S corporation. A child-care deduction would be allowed, however, as would a special adjustment for second wage earners in the same family. Personal exemptions would also be allowed and there would be a "zero-rate bracket" that would exempt a specified basic amount of income for each taxpayer.

Blueprints indicated that its model comprehensive income tax could raise the same revenue as the then-existing federal income tax if it had the following rates for joint returns:

Income bracket	Marginal tax rate (percent)
0–4,600	8
4,600–40,000	25
More than 40,000	38

The most widely mentioned of the comprehensive income tax proposals is the bill proposed by Senator Bill Bradley and Representative Richard Gephardt. Senators Mark O. Hatfield and Dan Quayle have also introduced comprehensive income tax proposals. Senator Quayle's would have perhaps the broadest tax base of all.[9] The tax base in Bradley-Gephardt would not be nearly so broad as in Quayle's bill. Bradley-Gephardt would retain the current $1,000 personal exemption for dependents, deductions for home mortgage interest, charitable contributions, state and local income and property taxes, and contributions to individual retirement accounts. The original Bradley-Gephardt proposal would have taxed the earnings in pension funds; their most recent one would not do this, but it would cut in half the upper limits on pension plan contributions: annual contributions would be reduced from $30,000 to $15,000, and the amount of

9. S. 1421, Fair Tax Act of 1983, by Sen. Bill Bradley, Democrat of New Jersey, and Rep. Richard Gephardt, Democrat of Missouri; S. 1040, Self-Tax Plan Act, by Sen. Dan Quayle, Republican of Indiana; and S. 2158, Simpliform Tax Act, by Sen. Mark Hatfield, Republican of Oregon.

the maximum pension that could be funded would be reduced from $90,000 to $45,000. They would retain the exclusion from income of veterans' benefits, social security benefits, and tax-exempt bond interest, as well as the exclusion of other government transfer payments. Their joint-return tax rates would be as follows:

Income bracket	Marginal tax rate (percent)
0–40,000	14
40,000–65,000	26
More than 65,000	30

However, the deductions for personal exemptions and itemized deductions (mortgage interest, taxes, and so on) would apply only against the 14 percent rate. The Bradley-Gephardt rates for income above $4,600 are much lower than those in *Blueprints*. Although the present income tax rates are also much lower than they were in 1977, when *Blueprints* was published, one wonders whether the Bradley-Gephardt base and rates would actually raise as much revenue as the present income tax.

Bradley-Gephardt would reduce the tax rate for corporations to 30 percent and would broaden the corporate tax base by eliminating the investment tax credit, slowing down depreciation, taxing U.S. parent corporations on the earnings of their foreign subsidiaries, taxing all gains in appreciated property distributed in liquidation of a corporation, and disallowing numerous other credits and deductions. The appeal of this kind of approach is obvious. As Senator Bradley points out, most Americans want lower rates, a simpler system, and an end to loopholes that other people use (but not, I would add, the ones they use) so that everyone pays a fair share of the tax. There are, however, a few problems that deserve attention.

Impact of the budget deficit. The comprehensive income tax rates that have been proposed are designed to produce the same amount of revenue as the present income tax. Senator Bradley goes even further, indicating that 70 percent of the individual taxpayers in America would pay less tax under his proposal than under present law. However, these rates cannot remain so low if we expect the income tax not only to provide as much revenue as it does today but to provide significant amounts of additional revenue. If the rates in Bradley-Gephardt and the other bills had to be increased to 20 percent, 39 percent, and 45 percent, respectively, for their three brackets, these bills would lose almost all of their appeal.

Can Congress adopt it? As one listens to the proponents of broad-based taxes describe the problems with the present system, one almost forgets that they are themselves members of Congress who have been there while it has all been happening. If they have not been able to keep the present income tax base simple, one must be skeptical that a truly meaningful base broadening could actually pass Congress. The present Congress, for example, has been utterly unable to come to grips with the question of how to treat fringe benefits.

Unless a significant change occurs in the way Congress operates, we must assume that even a new, comprehensive income tax would not be very broad or simple by the time it passed Congress, and that very soon it would be in much the same pickle as our present tax law. If this is so, one doubts that it can be worthwhile to undergo the substantial disruption in economic expectations which adoption of a radically new tax system would entail when the advantage would be small and so short-lived.

Impact on property values. The base broadening contemplated by the comprehensive income tax proposals will inevitably change the relative values of existing assets. For example, elimination of the capital gains preference should change the values of stocks and other assets that depend upon it as a significant element in their value. The disallowance of deductions for property taxes, home mortgage interest, or, as in Bradley-Gephardt, the reduction in their benefits, could alter the values of homes. The taxation of transfer payments could require governments to increase the amounts of those payments to maintain required levels of benefits. And so on. At the very least, significant grandfathering and transition rules would have to be adopted in order to prevent severe upsets in values and expectations. This will prevent the system from being very simple.

Creating regional differences. The economies of the different regions of the country take into account the existing tax systems. The disallowance of personal deductions for state taxes and interest may affect the residents of some regions more than others. For example, individuals living in a jurisdiction having high local taxes and high housing costs may be paying more state income, property, and sales taxes and interest than contemporaries in other jurisdictions. Such an individual lives on income net of these items; disallowing deductions for these items would hurt such persons more than it would those with similar net incomes who live in jurisdictions having lower local taxes and lower housing costs. This disparity would probably hurt the entire economy of high-tax states, whose residents are already adversely affected by the fact that deductions for state taxes are denied in computing the present alternative minimum tax.

Impact on savings. A comprehensive income tax is still an income tax, not a consumption tax, and these proposals would not eliminate the harm to saving that is inherent in any accretion tax. To the extent that the rates under a comprehensive income tax are lower than the rates under the present tax, the comprehensive income tax may be less detrimental to saving than the present tax. However, the elimination of the capital gains preference means that the tax rates on some aspects of investment will be higher rather than lower, and most of the proposals would reduce the deductions for individual retirement accounts and pension contributions (with some even taxing the income earned on pension funds). Thus, the comprehensive income tax proposals do not really solve the problem of the proper treatment of savings in our economy.

Effect on state tax systems. Although some of the proposals would eliminate itemized deductions for all forms of state and local taxation, others would discriminate among these forms. Some would allow a deduction for state income taxes but not for property and sales taxes; others would include a deduction for certain property taxes. When the state tax structure is examined from the vantage point of the state, however, all of these differing forms of tax are simply mechanisms for producing revenue for the conduct of state and local business. If deductions were permitted for certain types of state taxes but not others, one could predict that all of the states would adjust their tax systems to reduce or eliminate the nondeductible taxes and increase the others. This type of meddling with the autonomy of the states does not seem to be desirable. Thus, one would hope that the distinctions among state taxes would be eliminated in the comprehensive tax proposals and, because of the regional problems mentioned above, that all state and local taxes would continue to be deductible.

Cash Flow Consumption Taxes

The cash flow consumption tax would be collected much like the present income tax. As discussed in the Andrews article[10] and in the Treasury Department's *Blueprints,* this tax would be similar

10. Andrews, "A Consumption-Type or Cash Flow Personal Income Tax," pp. 113–19.

to an accretion tax except that it would be imposed only on the consumption portion and not on the accumulation portion of the accretion tax base. Individuals would still file tax returns. There would still be withholding on wages and the like. Income would be computed on a broad base much like those proposed for comprehensive income taxes (and, in addition, most loan proceeds would become income). But individuals would be able to deduct money contributed to qualified investment accounts, and the income on these investments would remain free of tax until spent on consumption. The latter result would be accomplished by bringing all investment proceeds (without reduction for cost basis) into ordinary income (there would be no special capital gains rate) and allowing a deduction for all investments. In effect, individuals could place in a giant individual retirement account all of their nonconsumption assets.

The cash flow consumption tax would have the advantage that it would not discriminate against savings. It would also treat people equally in the sense that people would pay tax based on their standard of living. However, there are significant problems inherent in the adoption of such a tax system as a substitute for our present income tax. Here are a few of them.

Lack of experience. A consumption tax of this kind has not been adopted by any other developed country. In fact, in the only countries where it has been tried, India and Sri Lanka, the tax has been a failure. We would be embarking on a largely untried experiment.

Weak distinction between investment and consumption. The tax depends upon one's ability to distinguish between investment and consumption, but the line between the two can be difficult to draw. How would one treat the purchase of valuable art to be hung in one's home, or the investment in a home or vacation property? All such items contain a mixture of investment and consumption aspects.

Need for a supplemental wealth tax. A cash flow consumption tax may be too favorable to accumulations of wealth. While a graduated consumption tax could become a progressive tax upon the standards of living actually enjoyed by differing individuals, there remains the fact that the mere ownership of invested wealth represents a tremendous advantage. The wealthy may be able to control business organizations and enjoy more power and auton-omy than the less wealthy, and they have the security of knowing that in the event of misfortune or retirement they will have sufficient assets to take care of themselves. I doubt very much that the American people would consider consumption alone to be a fair measure of the proper distribution of the tax burden in a system designed in part to reflect the concept of ability to pay. Moreover, to the extent that one purpose of the tax system is to prevent unreasonable accumulations of wealth, a cash flow consumption tax would have to be supplemented by a wealth tax or by sharply increased gift and estate taxes. But a wealth tax would not be possible without a constitutional amendment, and the valuation and administrative problems inherent in a wealth tax are not to be warmly embraced.

Transition problems. There would be difficult transition problems in moving from the present accretion tax system into a pure cash flow consumption tax system. Assets already owned by taxpayers at the time of the transition will have been subjected to one tax already, and it would be unfair to tax these once again when they are applied to consumption. For example, in a consumption tax system, when an investment asset that cost $1,000 is sold for $1,500 and the proceeds used for consumption, the full $1,500 gross proceeds are brought into income and taxed. Thus, as proponents of a cash flow consumption tax have all suggested, some kind of phasing-in process would be necessary to provide equity, and it would need to run for a number of years. This would greatly complicate the application of the system. (*Blueprints* even suggests that the income tax and the new consumption tax would both have to run simultaneously for a ten-year transition period, with the taxpayer having to pay the higher of the two taxes.) I doubt this is workable in the context of our present political system, because a system of transition set in force in the year of adoption of the new tax is unlikely to remain untouched by Congress for very long. And I doubt that the American people would stand for having to complete the forms for both taxes.

Most states have an income tax largely modeled on the federal tax. A shift from an income tax to a consumption tax at the federal level would affect the state tax systems as well, thereby intensifying the transition problems in moving from an income to a consumption tax system.

Difficulty in coordinating with foreign tax systems. Because a cash flow consumption tax has not been adopted by any developed country, our present international treaty system is based entirely on accretion income tax structures. The provisions of the tax codes of all of the developed countries are also written with a view to meshing with other accretion systems and not with a cash flow consumption tax. Under a cash flow consumption tax, we would have to restructure all of these provisions, a mammoth task that would substantially disrupt international transactions for some time.

Treatment of the corporate income tax. In pure theory, the corporate income tax has no proper place in a cash flow consumption tax system. In such a system the corporate tax should be eliminated, and tax should be imposed only at the individual level. Thus, proponents of a cash flow consumption tax have variously suggested that the corporate tax should be eliminated by integrating it with the individual income tax (in effect, using the corporation as a withholding vehicle) or that the corporate tax might be supplanted by a value-added tax or other consumption tax.

The problem with high rates. If a cash flow consumption tax were to provide not only as much, but even more revenue than our present individual income tax, the rates would have to be higher than individual income tax rates calculated on the same base. They would have to be higher still if the corporate tax were eliminated. How high they would have to be would depend in part on the breadth of the consumption base and on how much saving actually occurs. As mentioned earlier, the Treasury's estimates indicate that the rates for a broad-based cash flow consumption tax would not need to be much higher than the rates for a broad-based income tax, but this assumes that taxpayers will not greatly increase their saving.

Adverse impact on consumption. If an accretion tax discriminates against saving in relation to consumption, then it must follow (since this is its goal) that a consumption tax would do the opposite, that is, discriminate against consumption in relation to saving. But if American individuals were to reduce their consumption expenditures, this would most surely hurt the economy. Perhaps after a period of time this damage would be outweighed by the favorable result from greater capital investment in the economy, but in the meantime the decline in consumption could create economic disruption, which in turn could lead to short-term stimulative fiscal policies, greater deficits, and greater inflationary pressure.

Supplements to the present income tax

The other new taxes that are being discussed are excise taxes, the value-added tax, and a national retail sales tax. Like the cash flow consumption tax, these would shift our emphasis away from an accretion tax to a consumption tax. But unlike the cash flow consumption tax, these are supplements to, rather than substitutes for, our present income tax.

The Value-Added Tax

The value-added tax, unlike the cash flow consumption tax, is one with which there has been wide experience. For many years most of the industrial countries have successfully used a value-added tax as a major component of their tax systems. The typical value-added tax is very much like a national retail sales tax except that it is collected in a different fashion and tends in practice to have a much broader base than state and local retail sales taxes in the United States. Instead of being imposed only at the level of the final retail sale, the value-added tax is imposed at each level of production. For example, equipment and raw materials will be taxed upon sale to a manufacturer; the manufacturer in turn credits these taxes against those it must charge to the purchasers of its goods; and so on up and down the line.

The advantages claimed for a value-added tax are that it is a consumption tax and does not discourage saving; that it can be relatively simple; and that enforcement is relatively easy since each person in the chain of distribution acts as a tax collector, and fraud by one link in the chain is likely to have a relatively limited impact. Moreover, the value-added tax has obvious international advantages, since the General Agreement on Tariffs and Trade has allowed the tax to be rebated on export sales, something that cannot be done with income taxes. Thus, countries that derive a significant part of their revenue from the value-added tax are able to provide a kind of benefit for exports that countries like ours cannot easily match.

There are, however, the following significant drawbacks inherent in the adoption of a value-added tax.

High rates. For it to generate any significant amounts of revenue, not only must the value-added tax base be broad but the rates must be high. As mentioned earlier, it has generally been thought that each 1 percent of a broad-based value-added tax would produce revenues somewhere between $10 billion and $15 billion. Thus, to raise an additional $100 billion (without trying to substitute for the revenue now being raised by the individual income tax or the corporate income tax), the rate for the value-added tax would have to be somewhere between 6 percent and 10 percent. Individuals would still have to bear the burden of state and local sales taxes on top of this.

Initial "wealth tax" element. The adoption of a value-added tax might be viewed as a one-time wealth tax on all taxpaying individuals. If the rate were, say, 10 percent at the time of its adoption, the savings of all Americans would purchase only 91 percent of the goods that they could have purchased before the tax.

Simplicity. The sales taxes in most states have proven to be anything but simple. They are riddled with special rates and special exemptions. Given the propensities of our Congress, we should be skeptical about how simple any tax would be or would remain in our country.

Cost of compliance. The value-added tax imposes a tremendous burden upon those required to collect it, which would place a significant additional expense on the private sector of the American economy.

Discouragement of consumption. Because the value-added tax is a consumption tax, we can expect that, like a cash value consumption tax, it will discourage consumption. Indeed, we can expect that immediately before the adoption of any significant new consumption tax, there would be a flurry of buying, and after its adoption there would be a marked lull.

Intrusion on the states. Sales taxes have been an important source of revenue for state and local governments. Imposition of either a value-added tax or a national retail sales tax would place the federal government in competition with state and local governments for sales tax revenue. There is presumably some limit on how much aggregate sales tax can be imposed on any given transaction. The issue is, however, one of degree. Many of the federal excise taxes, such as the gasoline tax, can be viewed as sales taxes, and the simultaneous application of such excise taxes with state and local sales taxes has not been disruptive.

Encouragement of federal spending. The value-added tax would add a powerful new source of revenue for the federal government, and many people have considered this a reason for opposing rather than supporting such a tax. The concern is that after the income tax has reached a saturation point of acceptability, the adoption of a value-added tax will facilitate a significant increase in federal spending and thereby allow the government sector to absorb too much of the gross national product. When former House Ways and Means Committee Chairman Al Ullman introduced his proposal in 1979 for a reduced income tax coupled with a value-added tax, he proposed a limit on the proportion of GNP that the government could spend.[11] (Ullman proposed a limit of 22.6

11. See *Hearing Announcement on the "Tax Restructuring Act of 1979" (H.R. 5665)*, Committee Print, House Committee on Ways and Means, 96 Cong. 1 sess. (GPO, 1979).

percent for 1981, declining to 20 percent by 1986. We are significantly over those limits now: federal spending absorbed 25 percent of GNP in 1983.) Unless such a limit were adopted as a constitutional amendment, however, it would not be likely to have credibility. We have had a statutory limit on the federal debt ceiling each year during my lifetime, and it has never meant anything. Yet one should not lightly approach the adoption of constitutional limitations.

Regressivity. A value-added tax would be more regressive than a graduated income tax. Lower-income persons need to spend a larger proportion of their income on consumption than do the wealthy (although a good many wealthy persons choose to spend an equal proportion). Unless a value-added tax were complicated with various exemptions and credits (including credits against income tax), it would be essentially a flat-rate tax that would be proportional to an individual's consumption. While one could create a graduated-rate cash flow consumption tax, it would not be feasible for a value-added tax.

Impact on inflation. Income taxes are not taken into account in the various inflation indexes, whereas sales taxes are. Adoption of a value-added tax would have an immediate inflationary impact caused both by the change it would create in the indexes (which are used for purposes of many contract provisions) and by the tendency it would have to increase wage demands. Presumably the index portion of the problem could be solved simply by changing the index bases so as to neutralize the impact of the tax, but there would probably remain the inflationary impact from actual wage demands.

Lack of a pre-existing collection mechanism. The value-added tax in most European countries was a substitute for turnover taxes, and the shift to it was one of degree rather than kind. In contrast, the federal government has no existing machinery for collecting a value-added tax. It would have to start from scratch in preparing forms, issuing regulations, and establishing and training an inter-pretative and auditing force. This will involve expense and a certain amount of delay between adoption of a value-added tax and its commencement.

National Retail Sales Tax

The general impact of a national retail sales tax would be similar to that of a value-added tax. However, many students of the subject have concluded that the multiple layers of collection in a value-added tax tend to make evasion less easy than it would be under a national sales tax. The function of both taxes is to end up with a net tax on retail consumption and no tax on business investment. The value-added tax accomplishes this by imposing a tax at each level of purchase, and then allowing a credit for the earlier taxes to each person who adds value to a product before it reaches the ultimate consumer. The difference between consumption and purchase for business use is determined by the fact that the retail consumer simply has no sales subject to the value-added tax against which to credit the tax paid on his purchases. It is more difficult to distinguish between purchase for consumption and purchase for business use in the case of a retail sales tax. For example, when someone buys a typewriter, it is not always easy to tell whether the typewriter is to be used for personal rather than business purposes.

On the other hand, a value-added tax is more expensive to administer than a sales tax, because it involves many more levels of collection to raise the same net amount of tax. Because of this and because Americans have experience with sales taxes but not with a value-added tax, a national retail sales tax may prove more attractive.

The drawbacks to a value-added tax are also drawbacks to a sales tax. In addition, however, some observers believe it is easier to grant special exclusions or rates for particular types of transactions in a single-level sales tax than in a multilevel value-added tax and that a sales tax will thus end up being more complex.

In New York, the sales tax is one of the newer state taxes, and it has proven to be complex and difficult to enforce. There are exemptions based on the type of goods sold (for example, many grocery items and drugs are exempt, but other necessities like shoes and clothes are not), or on the use to which the goods will be put (such as the exemption of goods sold for resale), or on the nature of the transaction (certain casual sales by nondealers are exempt), or on the status of the purchaser (purchases by charities and certain others are exempt). Application of the tax requires hundreds of different judgments by retail establishments, and errors and inconsistencies are frequent. For example, cold nuts are exempt but heated nuts are taxable as a prepared food; most shampoos are taxable but some containing dandruff preventives are exempt as drugs; and so on. Because of the various exemptions, audit of the sales tax has proven difficult for New York. Physical review of every sales slip is not feasible, yet sampling methods are not wholly satisfactory either.

Energy Severance Taxes

We are raising roughly $13 billion per year from the windfall profits tax. A severance tax on fossil fuels, combined with an import tax on imported oil, could raise additional revenue.

Severance taxes are a province of the states. Residents of New York are acutely aware that states like Texas are able to run their state governments on energy source taxes that are largely paid by New Yorkers and other nonresidents of Texas. This allows Texas businesses and residents to enjoy a low state tax burden, thereby attracting citizens and businesses away from jurisdictions like New York. While Texans might not agree, I think this creates an unfair regional result. Congress should consider raising additional revenue by eliminating these regional discriminations and allowing energy source severance taxes to be imposed only at the federal level.

Summary

When former House Ways and Means Committee Chairman Al Ullman introduced his proposal for a value-added tax in 1979, he did so as part of a package in which the impact of the federal income tax would be reduced by amendments very similar to those that were actually adopted in the Economic Recovery Tax Act of 1981 (lowering rates, accelerating depreciation, improving savings incentives). The revenue gap would be filled by the value-added tax, and a ceiling would be imposed on the proportion of GNP that could be absorbed by the federal government. Ullman is widely believed to have lost his seat in Congress as a result of his espousal of the value-added tax. Since then, we have with the 1981 act adopted a significant reduction in the impact of the income tax, but after a concerted effort to reduce federal spending we are left with federal deficits of about $200 billion per year.

The enormity of the federal deficit colors everything. We have three choices: we can leave the level of federal revenue collection about where it is and drastically reduce spending for national defense, social security, and medicare;[12] we can reduce spending a little, increase tax revenues a little, and leave a significant federal budget deficit each year; or we can reduce spending substantially,

12. Federal budget outlays for 1984 are expected to be about $830 billion, of which $235 billion is for defense, $229 billion for social security and medicare, $101 billion for interest on the national debt, and $265 billion for "all other." Expenditures for the "all other" category have gone down significantly during the Reagan administration, while the others have increased significantly. See *Tax Notes* (February 27, 1984), p. 835. Thus any significant future expenditure reductions would seem to have to come from national defense and social security and medicare.

increase tax revenues substantially, and create a budget balance or surplus except for recession years. If we assume that the first alternative is impractical and that the second alternative is unwise, we are faced with the necessity of either replacing our present income tax with a much broader-based tax or of supplementing it with an entirely new federal tax or taxes.

The various new tax forms that might be considered for this purpose fall into two sharply different categories with respect to their impact on savings and capital formation. Given the rates that would have to be imposed if the necessary level of revenue were to be raised, a broad-based comprehensive income tax would seem to create a greater adverse effect on savings than our present income tax. On the other hand, consumption taxes would be more favorable to saving and capital formation.

The proposals also differ with respect to the disruption that they would create in present economic values and patterns of economic activity. Asset values generally reflect the expected flow of after-tax income that can be derived from them. Replacement of our present income tax by either a very broad-based comprehensive income tax or a cash flow consumption tax would disrupt these expectations; these two proposals might therefore be viewed as revolutionary rather than evolutionary changes in the tax structure. Transitional provisions to reduce the degree of disruption would complicate any new tax structure and would lower the amount of revenue that could be raised. Supplementing our present tax law by a new tax source such as energy taxes or a value-added tax would also disrupt present values, but one wonders if it would be quite as disruptive as the complete replacement of our income tax with a new system.

The other very important reality we must face is Congress's inability to protect our present income tax from complexity and its propensity to include special incentive and penalty provisions. If we were to assume from this reality that any broad-based comprehensive income tax would start out being not very simple and would soon be as complex as what we have now, we probably would not wish to pay the price of the initial economic disruption for such a dubious benefit. It might be better to work for more gradual, evolutionary changes in our income tax designed to broaden the base and improve the incentives for saving.

For my part, I would prefer to see the primary emphasis placed on spending reductions. The increase in federal spending during the last decade from about 20 percent to around 25 percent of GNP strikes me as unhealthy, especially when the burden of state and local taxes is counted. To the extent that sufficient spending reductions cannot be achieved, I would prefer to see the base of the present income tax expanded, though not at the expense of incentives for individuals to save (including individual retirement accounts and pension plans). Indeed, I would expand these. A temporary income tax surcharge is not a solution: our budget deficit is a long-term structural problem. If the deficit could not be eliminated by spending reductions and base broadening, I would move next to the imposition of federal energy taxes, and only if that did not solve the problem would I turn, reluctantly and as a last resort, to a value-added tax or national retail sales tax.

Considering the realities mentioned above, I would guess that the most likely course in the future will be some reduction in spending coupled with some base broadening and, I hope, improved savings incentives in our present tax system. But I suspect that these will not be enough to bring the deficit within tolerable levels and that Congress and the administration will supplement the income tax with additional excise taxes such as energy taxes and even perhaps a value-added or sales tax. Although the tilt toward consumption taxes (both through such changes in the income tax and through excise taxes) may be a salutary change, the probability of a heavier overall tax burden on the American people is quite discouraging.[13] How discouraged we should feel will depend on our ability to reduce spending for social security, medicare, and defense.

Comment by Byrle M. Abbin

BY PROCESS of elimination, Gordon Henderson reaches the conclusion that the income tax system should be continued but tied in with a value-added tax or some similar form of transactional consumption tax that provides greater revenue-generating capacity. He reluctantly comes to this conclusion, in spite of concerns about certain pragmatic problems that such a dual system might engender, including the very fundamental but enormous task of

---

13. See Keith Marsden, "Links between Taxes and Economic Growth: Some Empirical Evidence," *World Bank Staff Working Papers,* no. 605 (World Bank, 1983), which concludes from an initial study of twenty countries that those with low tax burdens experienced significantly better overall growth rates, including expansion of investment, productivity, and employment, and even a better distribution of income between the poor and the rich, than did those with high tax burdens.

educating the Internal Revenue Service and taxpayers to understand and work with a completely different system and mode of tax collection. The experiences of my European partners indicate that the pragmatic problems are more acute than Henderson suggests, and especially more consequential than most proponents of a value-added tax or a similar transactional consumption tax lead their listeners to believe. Former Commissioner of Internal Revenue Sheldon S. Cohen's remarks today aptly state his concern, based on information about evasion problems in the United Kingdom, where tax compliance is probably the best of any European country.

Value-added tax: administrative concerns

Henderson's exegesis of the many alternatives lays out the principal problems each poses. Additional problems that must be considered with a value-added tax are the following:

—The value-added tax is inherently inflationary and will work its way into cost-of-living adjustments. These adjustments may in turn directly affect entitlements such as social security or retirement benefits where cost-of-living adjustments are required by law or are of long-standing practice. To be sure, this impact can be factored out, but that may be through a mechanism that is complex and that could generate political problems. The addition of complexities to negotiations on union contracts also seems inevitable.

—In practice, considerably more administrative accounting tasks are imposed on the taxpayer who is the intermediary manufacturer, processor, marketer, or dispenser of goods or services, with no similar requirements for the ultimate individual purchaser. This adds complexity to the system.

—In every country with a value-added tax, a uniform flat rate has evolved into several different rates, depending on the nature of the merchandise or manufacture as well as the type of services. (Henderson has noted the overwhelming political temptation to provide special rules in the present system.) Certain special items are even exempted, so a significant amount of sorting of retail sales must occur.

—In practical application, everyone in the chain tends to experience a cash flow detriment since there is a delay between the payment made on sales to the next party in the manufacturing, wholesale, or retail chain and the offset that is allowed for the tax on purchases by that same business entity. For example, in France the cash flow delay is typically one month. These delays exacerbate the typically acute cash flow problems in start-ups where large purchases of fixed assets or inventory precede the build-up of sales volume. Where export sales are a heavy element of the total business transactions, delays also impinge on cash flow.

—In many jurisdictions the credits attributable to the tax imposed on the value that a company has added to a product are lost or very difficult to recover when bad debts arise from sales made by that company. This is so because the tax is imposed on the seller and not the buyer, an incidence difficult to change when bad debts are experienced.

—Sales of intangibles such as patents, copyrights, and royalties do not receive uniform treatment throughout the European Community. This has caused some confusion in trade among nations of the Community.

These few examples do not militate against implementing a value-added tax either as a supplement to the income tax or in lieu of it. Nevertheless, they represent problems that must be addressed if a value-added tax is to work efficiently and effectively.

The numbers Up to now the public discussion of alternative systems has been theoretical and based on considerations of fairness, simplicity, and equity, the standard-bearers of all the discussions about tax reform. Henderson has correctly pointed out that even confiscation of the assets of the wealthy would not solve the deficit problem. Some basic numbers underscore his point. They deserve attention in the process of evaluating alternatives such as base broadening, comprehensive income tax, and even a cash flow or accretion tax.

Contrary to the popular belief that the upper brackets pay little or no tax, the 1982 ratio of taxes to adjusted gross income for individuals in the $75,000–$100,000 range shows that their effective rate of taxation was nearly 25 percent and that effective rates increased to more than 39 percent for those with adjusted gross incomes of $1 million or more, according to the IRS's winter 1983–84 *Statistics of Income Bulletin*. By definition, adjusted gross income reflects income after business expenses but does not reflect any personal deductions such as home mortgage interest, real estate taxes, or charitable contributions. Obviously not shown in adjusted gross income are items such as the 60 percent excluded portion of long-term capital gains, tax-free interest, and deductions generated by tax-preferred investments (tax shelters). The average effective rate for $75,000 and above was 30.6 percent. This rate is noteworthy for two reasons. First, the effective rate for net taxable income (adjusted gross less personal deductions) would be substantially higher. Second, the rate is considerably higher than the flat 20 percent alternative minimum tax, suggesting that the incidence of preference use does not eliminate or reduce tax liability to nearly the degree that the public would like to believe.

If the 1982 effective rate had been increased to 50 percent, on a static basis, taxpayers with adjusted gross incomes of $200,000 or more would have paid an additional $10 billion annually, and those with $75,000 through $200,000 would have paid another $31 billion, for a total increase of $41 billion. This would have been a 65 percent increase over the current amount: a 104 percent increase for the $75,000–$100,000 range and a 72 percent increase for those in the $100,000–$200,000 range. Nonetheless, even those substantial amounts do not begin to solve the deficit problems. Clearly, there is no convergence of perception and reality when it comes to popular notions about the incidence of taxation among the "wealthy"; and "taxing the rich," a popular political slogan, will not make much of a dent in massive deficits.

The 1982 adjusted gross income of those who reported $75,000 of such income or more amounted to $208 billion, whereas the very narrow category of those earning between $50,000 and $75,000 adjusted gross income was $182 billion. The effective tax rate of the $50,000–$75,000 group was about 20 percent, and for incomes of more than $50,000 it was about 25 percent. This can hardly be characterized as massive tax avoidance, although, in theory at least, there is more room for taxation of the $50,000–$75,000 group.

The only point of this exercise is to show that there is only so much revenue that can be taxed from the upper middle class and wealthy. Personal living expenses and the itemized income tax deductions such as charitable, medical, and mortgage interest payments, as well as real estate and sales taxes, must still come from the residual adjusted gross income after tax. Thus it would seem that little is left beyond a 50 percent effective rate to amortize the current deficit, let alone to permit increased taxes for additional spending. It seems unlikely that the government could sustain current spending levels without significant increases in taxation at levels that go into the middle class and below. To be sure, some additional tax base is available through amounts currently excluded in whole or part from adjusted gross income, but it is debatable how significant that might be vis-à-vis the increase in revenues that apparently is desired in many quarters. Solutions to the problems in the tax system, then, are inextricably linked to the one issue that rarely comes up during the tax debate, namely, how much of the gross national product should the government collect via taxes for spending. Thus, the agenda of the public may be to simplify taxation, while the real political agenda may be to find relatively painless ways to raise taxes. After all, a new tax system is still limited by its ability to generate revenue from a finite, albeit large, economy.

The "flat tax"

Henderson's discussion glosses over a fundamental question that is also sidestepped by most politicians, a number of economists, and most journalists discussing the subject of tax overhaul. Very simply, what is a flat tax? Economists and politicians have attached this euphemism to a wide spectrum of broad-based income taxes, various forms of consumption tax, and something akin to an accretion tax (that is, a tax on economic income or accretion of income). The philosophy behind these various proposals and their impacts vary substantially, but nevertheless they have been broadly marketed under the aegis of a flat tax. In the process, the concepts have been misrepresented, especially in the news media. As a result, the public believes that a flat tax is a panacea that accomplishes fairness, equity, and simplicity with everybody apparently better off. In a time of deficit crisis, this is certainly a contradiction in terms!

Although not new, much of the recent impetus for a true flat tax came from the proposal by Robert Hall and Alvin Rabushka. These Stanford (Hoover Institution) economists have heavily promoted their plan as one that allows taxes for both individuals and corporations to be completed on a postcard. The basic concept has been introduced in a bill (S. 557) by Senator Dennis DeConcini. For individuals, this is a true labor tax (although its authors describe it as a consumption tax), since a flat 19 percent rate is applied to salaries, with no deductions allowable. No other sources of income are taxed (thus investment gains are tax free), nor are deductions permitted for interest paid on borrowings.

Businesses would pay tax on their earnings on an unconsolidated basis. They could not deduct any remittances to borrowers or shareholders in the form of interest or dividends; thus, interest and dividend payments would be completely outside the tax system, since they would be neither taxable to the recipient nor deductible to the payer. Double taxation is eliminated, and a single, integrated system through a tax at the corporate level is achieved. In essence, the corporate tax would be like a form of withholding with no reporting by the recipient.

Obviously, a true flat tax such as Hall-Rabushka has its regressive aspects. To date, however, the public debate does not seem to have distinguished the dichotomy between the fairness issues raised by simplification and the fairness issues raised by equity in any true flat tax. As the public becomes more aware of that dichotomy, then it seems inevitable that the debate will take on political overtones as the winners and losers come to understand the effects of a true flat rate on their particular circumstances.

In tallying winners and losers, a much greater unknown will be the economic effect of the loss of deductions. Many commentators note that substantial phase-in considerations arise because a flat tax is such an abrupt departure from the current system. Hall and Rabushka conclude that interim valuation adjustments (that is, reduction to the "appropriate" level) based on neutrality among investments are the necessary costs of getting to a system that is better designed to generate savings. It is hard to imagine that this valuation adjustment period will be anything less than chaotic.

Another approach, presented by Senator Jesse Helms (S.Res. 205), should be noted. It is a very broad-based income tax, more correctly called a comprehensive income tax, deleting most current preferences (deductions, exclusions, and credits). Special treatment for capital gains is eliminated, and other forms of income that are currently partially or totally exempt would be taxed. Gifts and inheritances would be included in the tax base, so beneficiaries and recipients would be subject to an annual tax with no provision for current estate and gift deductions and credits. This new, expanded base would be subject to a flat 10 percent rate. (A similar proposal by Congressman Leon Panetta [H.R. 2520] is slightly less comprehensive and taxes at a 19 percent rate.) Like the Hall-Rabushka proposal, its simplicity in operation must be considered in light of the attendant significant transitional problems.

The most recent version of a flat tax was introduced by supply-siders, Congressman Jack Kemp and Senator Bob Kasten. The "Fair and Simple Tax of 1984" (S. 2600, H.R. 5533) would dramatically simplify the present system by broadening the base substantially and lowering the rate to 25 percent for individuals. However, the plan would retain many popular deductions, including mortgage interest, charitable contributions, accelerated cost recovery, and the tax-favored treatment of retirement savings and fringe benefits. The investment tax credit and other credit incentives would be eliminated. The Kemp-Kasten plan addresses the inherent regressivity issue with a special exclusion: 20 percent of salary in the social security wage base (now slightly in excess of $39,000) would be excluded and not subject to the flat 25 percent rate. As income rises above the wage base, the excluded portion would be added back into the tax base.

The "fair tax"

In contrast to a true flat tax, the most publicized of all the proposed changes to the income tax system is the Bradley-Gephardt "Fair Tax of 1983" (S. 1421). It has been mistakenly categorized as a flat-rate income tax. Their proposal is a significant adjustment of our current income tax system, eliminating most preference items (deductions, exclusions, and credits) but allowing the more politically popular deductions for charitable contributions, mortgage interest payments, state income and real estate taxes, and individual retirement account contributions. Interestingly, these deductions are reflected in the tax calculation at only the flat rate of 14 percent, the lowest bracket available in taxing income, so the deductions effectively become 14 percent credits no matter what the taxpayer's bracket. Individuals earning above the 14 percent taxable base of $25,000 are subject to two additional tax brackets of 26 percent and 30 percent. Thus, the Fair Tax is simply not a flat tax. Compared with present law, it is a broader-based income tax with fewer brackets and with the politically sensitive deductions allowed as flat-rate credits at the lower rate.

The current Bradley-Gephardt proposal purportedly does not generate more revenue than current law; but it obviously shifts the tax incidence to those who now use current tax advantages such as capital gains deductions and accelerated cost recovery to obtain tax reductions that would be eliminated if the Fair Tax were enacted. Moreover, there would be no indexing of rates to neutralize the impact of inflation. Like the true flat tax, transitional problems and economic displacements mar this approach. Since the current version of the Fair Tax is designed to be revenue neutral, it cannot solve deficit problems.

As can be seen, there are vast differences in the economic and political philosophies behind these different types of revenue approaches, all of which have been categorized and lumped together as forms of flat tax. The transitional problems (some of which are discussed by other commentators) required to avoid the consequences of abrupt changes lead me to agree with Henderson that the current budgetary needs are better met through, at most, a modification (and not a complete overhaul) of the current income tax system, complemented with a form of transaction tax to provide the necessary revenue increase.

Conclusion   In summary, more thought must go into the pragmatic implications of some of the proposals, whether they involve moving to new systems or to systems that are untried in the United States but that have exhibited administrative problems as well as abuse elsewhere. More attention must be given to the impact on the individual's economic situation flowing from the change, even though this may create another monster with two tax systems going along concurrently for several years. Before drastic changes are enacted, an increase in the budget of the Internal Revenue Service should be considered for additional employees to better police the current system. Enhanced enforcement would capture a greater share of underreported and nonreported items in the underground economy. More extensive withholding could be implemented to collect tax payments that do not get picked up through the self-assessment system.

None of the proposals offered so far to improve the tax system is a panacea, and none would be as simple in operation as it is in proposal form; each would likely take on political baggage as Congress faced the challenges of transition to the new system.

A Tax on Consumption, Gifts, and Bequests and Other Strategies for Reform

HENRY J. AARON *and* HARVEY GALPER

A CONSENSUS is developing that the federal income tax requires fundamental revision. The realization is widespread that a large increase in revenues will be needed to balance the budget. At the same time there is pervasive discontent about the structure of both personal and corporation income taxes.

We believe that this discontent is justified, in large part because both the personal and the corporation income taxes now embody conflicting principles of taxation. Some aspects of our tax system are consistent with the principle that all *income,* the sum of consumption plus additions to net worth, should be subject to tax. Other provisions embody the principle that savings and interest earnings on those savings should not be taxed until they are realized or consumed, an approach sometimes referred to as *expenditure* or *consumption* taxation. And a growing number of provisions comport with no consistent set of tax principles at all. These inconsistent principles are objectionable not because they are intellectually confused but because they lead to complexity, encourage tax avoidance, and promote decisions that are economically inefficient.

This situation has arisen gradually. Each new tax bill in recent years has contained a list of new provisions designed to achieve narrowly defined objectives. Although many of these objectives taken alone have considerable merit, the attempt to achieve them through the tax code has resulted in complexity and confusion.[1] As the most recent example, the Economic Recovery Tax Act of 1981 (even as modified by the Tax Equity and Fiscal Responsibility Act of 1982) moved in the direction of expenditure tax rules by providing cost recovery allowances that are close to expensing depreciable capital investments; the allowances are intended as an

The authors thank Gail Morton for research assistance and Alan Auerbach, Larry Dildine, Daniel Frisch, Daphne Greenwood, Daniel Halperin, Charles Hulten, Robert Lucke, Richard Musgrave, Joseph A. Pechman, Emil Sunley, and Eric Toder for critical and constructive comments.

1. See Richard Goode, "Lessons from Seven Decades of Income Taxation," this volume.

additional incentive to business investment and as an offset to inflation-related erosion of depreciation deductions. Unfortunately, the new rules are inconsistent with income tax rules regarding the deductibility of interest expenses. The net result is an expansion of tax-related distortions in the allocation of business investment and magnified opportunities for tax avoidance.

At the same time that inconsistencies are proliferating in the tax system, recognition is growing that high marginal tax rates distort economic decisions. The movement to lower marginal rates began in earnest with the 1964 tax act, which cut the top marginal personal income tax rate from 91 to 70 percent. Additional steps were taken in 1969, when the top rate on earned income was reduced to 50 percent, and in the 1981 act, when the top rate on other income was also cut to 50 percent. However, because the lower rate structure enacted in 1981 was not accompanied by a broadening of the tax base, the most dramatic effect of the recent tax legislation was a huge reduction in federal revenues. Under current economic assumptions, the 1981 and 1982 acts in combination reduced fiscal 1985 revenues by $129 billion and reduced fiscal 1989 revenues by $274 billion.[2] As a result, the United States is now in a position where it must raise revenues by about $100 billion (the exact amount depends on the size of cuts in defense and nondefense spending) but where simply increasing rates will aggravate already serious distortions arising from an almost capriciously defined tax base.

Clearly, a thorough reexamination of current U.S. tax policy is required. We have written this paper in the hope that an evaluation of alternative ways of raising $100 billion by 1989 will contribute to such a reexamination. We acknowledge that new revenue sources—a more extensive use of specific excises or a broad-based sales or value-added tax—are possible revenue-raising candidates. But we assume that much of the added revenue will come from personal and business income taxes; especially if this assumption is correct, but even if it is not, it is vital that amendments to the tax code be founded on the touchstones of public finance: equity, economic efficiency and growth, and ease of administration.

In this paper we shall explore the implications for tax reform that would arise from adherence to these too-often ignored principles. The first section examines how the principles should

---

2. Congressional Budget Office, *Baseline Budget Projections for Fiscal Years 1985–1989* (Government Printing Office, February 1984), table D, p. 116.

be used to guide structural tax reform. The succeeding sections apply the principles to four alternative ways of increasing revenues that have received widespread support. We pay most attention to a proposal that would base tax liability on the present value of total lifetime resources.

Principles of tax reform

Tax reform should be guided by the principles of fairness, economic efficiency and growth, and ease of administration. In practice, of course, no system can completely realize all of these partly conflicting goals. For example, complete fairness would require recognition of the many characteristics of particular persons and businesses, but cluttering the tax code with numerous special provisions increases costs of compliance and enforcement. Of perhaps greater importance, people are certain to have different views about what is fair, enforceable, and conducive to growth, and about the relative importance of these goals. The legislative result of any reform program will reflect compromises among these goals and is unlikely to match any ideal precisely.

Most people understand that many sources or uses of income are not fully taxed, and this realization underlies cries for reform. But they also think that the current personal and corporation income taxes, for all their imperfections, are just that—taxes on income. The facts are rather different. For example, although interest income received directly by individuals is usually fully taxed, as required under an income tax, the tax on interest income paid into such sheltered accounts as Keogh plans, individual retirement accounts, and qualified pension plans is deferred until withdrawal. Such deferral is close to the principles of a personal consumption tax, under which income is taxed only if it is consumed but not if it is saved.

The coexistence of rules that express contrary tax principles causes serious problems. For example, individuals can shift assets from taxable to tax-sheltered accounts, saving nothing but avoiding tax nevertheless. They can also borrow money, take deductions for the interest paid on the loan, and deposit the funds in a sheltered account, interest on which is not taxed currently. In both cases, tax provisions promoted to increase saving result in tax avoidance but no net saving. The two cases illustrate the problems that arise because our current tax rules combine elements of income-type and of consumption-type taxes.

Two crucial choices must be made in charting a program of structural tax reform. First, should direct personal and business taxes remain the principal sources of federal revenues? Or should increased reliance be placed on commodity taxes such as a value-added tax or selected excises? Second, should the personal tax on individuals and the tax on businesses be based on the principle that all income should be taxed? Or should it be based on the principle that consumption should be taxed, with savings or investments exempt until consumed or transferred to others?

In fashioning structural tax reform, the choice between moving to the comprehensive income tax or to the personal consumption tax should not hinge on the mistaken belief that the present system closely resembles one or the other or that it would be significantly easier to attain one than the other. The present tax system is far removed from both, and the attainment of either will involve wrenching decisions. But these decisions cannot be avoided if we are to reduce the needless inequities and inefficiencies of the present system.

Fairness

Fairness requires that people in equal circumstances pay the same tax.[3] The practical problem is how to define "equal circumstances" and "same tax."

According to the most widely accepted definition, two individuals are in equal circumstances if, during a given period of time (usually one year), each person's consumption plus additions to net worth is the same.[4] Under this principle the tax base should include all earnings and all accrued capital income whether it is realized or not. In practice, the present tax system violates this principle in myriad ways.

Inflation. First, proper application of the principle requires that all quantities be measured in real terms with full adjustments for inflation.[5] The measurement of real labor income usually presents

3. The issue of fairness also involves the relative tax burdens paid by people in unequal circumstances, which is the question of how progressive the tax system should be. We intend to put this issue aside for the present. It should be debated fully once the tax base has been redefined.

4. A strong argument can be made that this definition is logically flawed because it ignores the value of leisure. Thus, persons A and B, with equal skills, earning opportunities, and asset income, may make different decisions about how hard to work. Person A is paid at a high hourly wage and spends the income by consuming costly vacations and durable goods. Person B works part time, earns enough to live on, and enjoys an easy life consuming leisure. It is arguable that persons A and B should not be taxed differently because ex ante they are in equal circumstances. Whatever the appeal of an ex ante definition of income (and even that is debatable), there is no way to apply it. Taxes must be imposed ex post on actual outcomes.

5. Automatic adjustments of tax brackets enacted in 1981 concern the calculation of tax rates by income class but have nothing to do with measurement of the tax base. Rate indexation could be achieved by annual tax legislation; but indexation of the base can be achieved only if tax accounting rules are fundamentally changed to prevent inflation from distorting the measurement of taxable income.

few problems. However, correct measurement of capital income during periods of inflation is complex. The value of depreciation deductions is eroded by inflation. The measurement of capital gains or losses is distorted when the value of dollars received at sale differs from that of dollars used to acquire the asset. Interest on loans may be partly or completely offset by changes in the real value of the loan repayment. Full adjustment of all these quantities is possible but difficult, and there is even disagreement in principle about how far such adjustments should go.[6]

Accrual or realization. In principle, the income tax rests on the "accretion" concept that consumption plus additions to net worth in each period constitutes the correct measure of ability to pay. This concept means that capital gains should be taxed as they accrue, for that is when they add to ability to pay. Taxing all capital gains as they accrue is impossible, which means that the income tax is inequitable by its own standard.

For example, if person A enjoys a capital gain or suffers a capital loss on a retained asset, the tax payment is not affected by that gain or loss. If person B experiences the same gain or loss and sells the asset, the tax payment is affected. If person C has two assets, one of which appreciates and one of which declines in value by the same amount, the total economic income from both assets is zero. But if person C sells the asset that has declined in value and retains the appreciated asset, the tax collector observes a loss for the year, and the individual is able to enjoy a tax reduction by subtracting part or all of this loss from other income. Taxpayers thus can reap the benefits of immediate deductions by realizing accrued losses while letting accrued gains accumulate.

The taxation of capital gains as realized raises other problems. Because capital gains tend to be "lumpy"—the accumulated gain of many years is often realized in one year—they may push people into much higher tax brackets. For this and other reasons the current tax system imposes lower rates on long-term capital gains than on most other income. Alternatively, capital gains could be averaged over several years in any of several different ways.[7]

6. For example, when expected inflation increases, nominal interest rates tend to rise, causing the market value of outstanding bonds to decline. The decline in the market value of a firm's debt represents an accrued capital gain to the firm and an accrued capital loss to its bondholders in the year during which they occur. Should these gains and losses be recognized by the tax system? These gains and losses will be reversed as the bonds approach maturity. It would be difficult in practice to distinguish such fluctuations in bond prices from those caused by changes in the creditworthiness of the issuing firm.

7. For example, if an asset is held ten years, one could calculate the additional tax in the year the gain is realized on one-tenth of the gain and collect ten times that amount.

Saving versus consumption. When individuals can control the timing of consumption over successive periods, large inequities may result. A numerical example illustrates these relations. Persons A and B both earn 100 in period 1. The income of person A is consumed as it is earned. All the income of person B is saved and invested at the prevailing rate of 20 percent. In period 2, person B cashes and consumes the investment made in period 1. Person C earns 120 in period 2 and consumes it immediately.

Without taxes, persons A and B have exactly the same consumption opportunities: to consume 100 immediately or 120 in period 2. In fact, if person C can borrow in period 1 against period 2 income at the same interest rate persons A and B earn on their investments, person C too would be able to consume 100 in period 1 or 120 in period 2. However, under current income tax rules (assuming for this example a 20 percent tax rate), A pays a tax of 20 in period 1 and nothing in period 2; B pays 20 in period 1 and 3.2 (on the return of 16 from saving 80) in period 2; and C pays 24 in period 2. Despite their equal consumption opportunities, B pays higher taxes in present-value terms than either A or C.[8]

Because all three persons have the same spending opportunities, we hold that it is only fair to tax them equally. This goal can be achieved in this example in either of two ways: by taxing all earnings or by taxing all consumption. If all earnings are taxed at, say, 10 percent, persons A and B would both pay tax of 10 in period 1, and person C would pay tax of 12 in period 2. If all consumption (including tax payments) is taxed at the same rate, person A pays a tax of 10 in period 1, and persons B and C pay a tax of 12 in period 2. In both cases the tax liabilities of all three persons are equivalent, because liabilities of 12 in period 2 have a value of 10 in period 1 if they are discounted at a 20 percent interest rate.

An additional complication must be taken into account. Suppose that person B decides not to consume any savings but to bequeath or give them to a relative. If bequests, gifts, and inheritances are not counted in the tax system, the alternative approaches of taxing earnings or taxing consumption are no longer equivalent as long as the earnings of each person are not all consumed. If only earnings were taxed, it would be possible for people with large

---

More generally, the tax on capital gains could be set at n times the incremental tax on $1/n$ of the gain, where n is the holding period in years.

8. At a 20 percent before-tax discount rate, the taxes of A and C are equal in present value. At an after-tax discount rate of 16 percent, C's taxes exceed those of A.

inheritances to consume out of their inherited wealth without incurring any tax liability in their lifetime. If the tax were based only on consumption, it would be possible for those earning substantial sums to avoid much tax in their lifetimes by bequeathing large estates to their heirs. The failure to include gifts and bequests is inconsistent with the principle that tax burdens should be a function of ability to pay. The tax base must explicitly include gifts and bequests made in the tax base of the donor or decedent and gifts and inheritances received in the tax base of the beneficiary.

It is possible to deal with inheritances and bequests in either of two ways. Taxes could be imposed on all earnings plus inheritances or on all expenditures, including bequests and other transfers. If the first approach is taken, persons with equal earnings who saved equal amounts but who earned widely varying rates on their saving would all pay the same tax. This ex ante approach would levy taxes on initial opportunities or expected returns from saving rather than on actual outcomes. Alternatively, all outlays, including bequests and other transfers, could be taxed. This ex post approach would impose taxes on actual outcomes rather than initial opportunities. Because actual rates of return differ enormously, we believe that the ex post approach would generally be regarded as much fairer.[9]

Economists should recognize that the expenditure tax base is simply the familiar Haig-Simons definition of income extended from one year to the lifetime and expressed in present value terms. This variant of the Haig-Simons definition of income is exactly equivalent to the base of a personal expenditure or consumption tax that treats bequests and gifts to others as consumption. Because of its similarity to the *annual* Haig-Simons income tax, we shall refer to it as a *lifetime* income tax, because it would tax total consumption plus change in net worth over an individual's lifetime.[10]

Averaging and the accounting period. If tax rates are progressive

9. The current system, which uses actual rather than expected income, is based on the second approach.

10. This tax might also be called an "endowment" tax, because the base is the capacity of each person to spend over the course of his or her lifetime. It is not the same as a consumption tax that falls only on consumption and excludes changes in net worth by exempting gifts and bequests from the tax base. See Richard A. Musgrave, "ET, OT, and SBT," *Journal of Public Economics,* vol. 6 (July–August 1976), pp 3–16; and Musgrave, "The Nature of Horizontal Equity and the Principle of Broad-based Taxation: A Friendly Critique," in John G. Head, ed., *Taxation Issues of the 1980s* (Melbourne: Australian Tax Research Foundation, 1983), pp. 21–33. For measures of the effects on a cash flow tax of excluding bequests and gifts, see Paul L. Menchik and Martin David, "The Incidence of a Lifetime Consumption Tax," *National Tax Journal,* vol. 35 (June 1982), pp. 189–203.

and taxes are levied annually (or for any other period shorter than the taxpayer's lifetime), tax liability will depend not only on the total of consumption plus gifts and bequests but also on the pattern of these flows. The more uneven the flows, the greater the tax liability under any given set of progressive rates. This problem is far more serious under the present personal income tax than it would be under the lifetime income tax, because income fluctuates more than consumption does.[11]

To deal with this problem under the present income tax, the law permits limited averaging. Averaging ameliorates the effects of some short-term fluctuations in income, but it does nothing to reduce the distortions arising from life-cycle variations in income. Although the base for the lifetime income tax is a superior measure of individual capacity to spend and tends to vary less from year to year than the current base, distortions might still arise if no allowance were made for annual variations. Later in the paper we will examine the possibilities for such an allowance.[12]

Efficiency and Growth

Taxes should distort as little as possible economic decisions that would have been made in the absence of taxation.[13] The principle of minimizing distortions also presumes that the choices made in the absence of taxes would result in profit and personal satisfaction

11. A large body of research on consumer behavior has established that consumers tend to base outlays on normal income, perceptions about which oscillate less than income does. These research findings define consumption as the flow of services from consumer goods. Except for large expenditures on high-cost consumer durables, such as automobiles and housing, the difference between consumption expenditures and services of consumer goods are seldom important. Because of their size, consumer purchases of housing and automobiles require special treatment if consumption plus gifts and bequests is the tax base.

12. If the entire tax schedule is changed from time to time, fluctuations in the annual tax base can cause inequities for reasons similar to those that arise because rates are progressive. Persons with relatively high-consumption years in high-tax periods pay more tax than those with relatively low consumption in those periods. To the extent that persons of similar ages are involved, the self-averaging of consumption relative to income reduces this problem of tax base volatility, and the explicit averaging provisions to be discussed later in the text reduce it still further. To the extent that inequities arise because members of one cohort worked during a low-wage period, such as the Great Depression, or in high-tax periods, such as World War II, the tax system cannot resolve them. These intercohort inequities can only be dealt with if they are addressed explicitly. For example, one justification for the generous treatment of the aged under social security during the early years of that program has been that they suffered disproportionately (and with little hope of recoupment) from the economic deprivations of the depression of the 1930s.

13. This principle is stated in recognition of the fact that nondistorting lump-sum taxes cannot equitably raise sufficient revenue to support the activities of modern governments. All other taxes affect some important economic decision—how much to save or to work, what to consume, or which investments to undertake.

greater than would result from any other set of choices. This is the principle that underlies reliance on market allocation of resources.[14]

Few of the distortions arising from the present tax system can be justified on the ground that they offset natural inefficiencies. First, broad classes of savings and investments are subject to widely varying effective tax rates.[15] Second, the personal decision about whether to save or to consume is distorted by the treatment of saving.[16]

Investment distortions. Table 1 shows that the effective rates of tax on different classes of investments vary from 91.2 percent to −16.3 percent (the latter therefore a subsidy rather than a tax) depending on type of asset, industry, source of finance, and type of ownership. The table does not show that, within these categories, the range of effective tax rates is even wider, from 111 percent on buildings financed by new shares sold to households in either manufacturing or commerce, to −105 percent on machinery used in the commercial sector financed by debt sold to tax-exempt institutions.[17]

These variations in effective tax rates arise because of the interactions of several features of the tax system. (1) Tax depreciation bears little relation to true economic depreciation. (2) The investment tax credit is available only on certain assets. (3) Effective tax rates are sensitive to the method of finance and to the tax status of the owner of the financing instrument or the capital asset. (4) Both personal and corporate taxes must be paid on corporate-source income but only personal taxes on business income from noncorporate sources. (The taxing of financial institutions poses its own special problems.) The failure of our tax system to adjust the measurement of capital income for inflation increases all these distortions.

14. Important exceptions to this principle occur when actions of one person or business affect others, and no market exists to take these effects into account; when buyers or sellers lack important information and cannot obtain it easily; and in certain other circumstances. In such cases, tax measures that distort private decisions may improve economic efficiency by offsetting private-sector errors. For example, it may improve efficiency to impose a tax in order to raise the price of goods that produce harmful byproducts. Such price increases would discourage consumption and production of such goods.

15. Mervyn A. King and Don Fullerton, eds., *The Taxation of Income from Capital: A Comparative Study of the United States, the United Kingdom, Sweden, and West Germany* (University of Chicago Press, 1984).

16. Martin Feldstein, "The Welfare Cost of Capital Income Taxation," *Journal of Political Economy*, vol. 86 (April 1978), pp. S29–S52.

17. King and Fullerton, *Taxation*, pp. 299–300.

Table 1. Effective Marginal Tax Rates on Investment, by Asset, Industry, Source of Finance, and Owner, 1980

Percent

Investment category	Effective marginal tax rate
Type of asset	
Machinery	17.6
Building	41.1
Inventories	47.0
Industry	
Manufacturing	52.7
Other industry	14.6
Commerce	38.2
Source of finance	
Debt	−16.3
New share issues	91.2
Retained earnings	62.4
Owner of asset	
Households	57.5
Tax-exempt institutions	−21.5
Insurance companies	23.4
All investments	37.2

Source: Mervyn A. King and Don Fullerton, *The Taxation of Income from Capital: A Comparative Study of the United States, the United Kingdom, Sweden, and West Germany* (University of Chicago Press, 1984), p. 244.

The costs of tax-related distortions can be large. Suppose that the tax law distinguishes three types of investments: type A investments, taxed at 80 percent; type B investments, 40 percent; and type C investments, zero percent. If these investments are equally risky, investors will want to earn the same after-tax return from each investment. If type C investments yield 6 percent before and after tax, type B investments will have to earn 10 percent before tax, and type A investments will have to earn 30 percent if funds are put into all three types of investments. As a result, a type A investment that yields, say, 29 percent before tax will lose out to a type C investment that yields only 6 percent. Nearly four-fifths of the potential return on the marginal dollars of investment would be lost because of distortions induced by the tax system. Not all misallocations attributable to the tax system are as extreme as this example, but some are worse. And although most empirical estimates of the losses from tax-induced distortions in the allocation of capital are much smaller than this example would suggest, none of the estimates has taken full account of the distortions induced by the entire tax system.

Distortion of consumption and saving. Like investments, the form of household saving is distorted by wide variations in the tax treatment of asset income. Payments into, and income earned on, qualified pensions and individual retirement accounts are untaxed until withdrawn. Interest on municipal bonds is untaxed at any time. Gains in the value of assets are untaxed until realized and are never taxed if the holder dies before realizing them. Up to $125,000 of capital gain on owner-occupied housing is exempted from tax if the owner does not realize the gain until the age of fifty-five or later. In contrast, interest on corporate and federal debt and most dividends are taxed in full if received by households. Although the treatment of asset income is highly varied, expenses incurred in earning this income, including interest, are usually deductible.

These inconsistent rules produce a pattern of wealth holding quite different from what would appear optimal in their absence. In the pursuit of tax advantages, individuals may sacrifice liquidity or vary the degree of risk that they are willing to assume. Furthermore, households may be able to obtain tax benefits merely by changing the form of their saving or by borrowing in order to save in a tax-preferred form. It is even possible for current tax law to make profitable an investment that would be unprofitable in the absence of taxes.[18]

In addition to distorting the form of saving, the income tax also discourages people from providing for future consumption needs. When one earns a dollar, one must decide whether to consume it now or to save it for later consumption or bequest. If there were no taxes, this decision would be based on present wants, one's best guess about future wants, and the rate of return on savings. The personal income tax distorts this decision, because the return on savings is taxed. As a result the income tax increases

18. Consider a tax-exempt investment yielding 8 percent and a borrowing cost of 12 percent. In the absence of tax distortions, it would not make sense to borrow money to buy such a tax-exempt investment because the investor would lose 4 percent. A taxpayer in the 50 percent bracket can make a profit by such a transaction, however. Such a taxpayer can borrow at 12 percent and, because the net cost after deducting interest expenses is only 6 percent, can make 2 percent on the investment. The Internal Revenue Code contains provisions designed to discourage such loans, but they are easy to avoid. See Harvey Galper and Eugene Steuerle, "Tax Incentives for Saving," *Brookings Review,* vol. 2 (Winter 1983), pp. 16–23.

the cost of future consumption or, in other words, reduces the reward to savings.

The discouragement to future consumption can be large. Suppose a thirty-year-old person is considering whether to consume income currently or to save it for retirement consumption thirty-five years later. Assume that the annual rate of return on savings is 10 percent. In the absence of taxes, this person must give up $35 of current consumption for each $1,000 to be spent in retirement.[19] In the presence of a 30 percent tax, this person must give up $94 of current consumption for the same end.[20] The income tax system nearly triples the amount of current consumption that must be surrendered for future income security and thereby discourages people from providing for themselves.

The lifetime income tax would not produce such an effect. The amount of current consumption that would have to be surrendered to finance consumption in the future would be the same as it would be without taxes.[21] Thus the lifetime income tax would not only comport with principles of fairness but would also terminate tax-induced distortions in saving.

Some argue that greater incentives to save would result under the expenditure tax than result under the current income tax and that this fact is a major argument for expenditure-type taxes. Although we agree that the incentive to save would increase, we do not consider that prospect a major argument on behalf of expenditure-type taxes. The increases in the rates of saving and capital formation would contribute to economic growth, but the increases would be small relative to those that could be achieved by another, readily available instrument: a fiscal policy to reduce the deficit or to create a surplus.[22] The tax system should be

19. For example, in the absence of taxes, the person who earned $1,000 at age thirty could consume $1,000 currently or invest it at 10 percent for thirty-five years, accumulate $28,102, and consume the proceeds. The price of each dollar of retirement consumption, as measured by the amount of first-period consumption that must be surrendered to get $1 of retirement consumption, is $0.0356 (1,000/28,102 = 0.0356).

20. The income tax would reduce the net rate of return from 10 percent to 7 percent. At 7 percent compound interest $94 accumulates to $1,000 after thirty-five years.

21. If there is a tax of, say, 30 percent, the example in note 20 is modified in this way: the person has a choice between consuming $700 currently and investing the $1,000 at 10 percent, realizing $28,102 after thirty-five years, and consuming $19,672 ($28,102 less 30 percent tax). The price per dollar of retirement consumption is again $0.0356 (700/19,762 = 0.0356), the same as in the no-tax case.

22. Household saving has run at about 3.5 percent of GNP in recent years. Even if such saving increased by about one-third—a decidedly generous estimate—the effect on *national* saving would be a small fraction of the direct and certain effects of eliminating the federal deficit, which is projected to rise to 6 percent of GNP.

designed to be fair, conducive to efficient use of resources, and easily administered. An increase in saving would be an incidental consequence of these other reforms.

Ease of Administration

Collecting taxes is costly. Taxpayers have to spend time and money figuring out what they owe. Tax authorities have to make sure that taxes owed are actually paid. Getting these costs down is an important goal of tax reform.

As the complexity of the personal and corporate income taxes has grown, compliance costs have risen correspondingly. Complex rules, combined with inflation, have increased opportunities for tax avoidance. But taking full advantage of these opportunities takes careful, and often costly, planning and expert advice. An industry has grown up to help people arrange their affairs to minimize the taxes they owe. Another industry has arisen to help people fill out their returns. Over 40 percent of individual tax returns are now filled out with the assistance of a professional tax preparer.[23] The result of all this activity has little if any social value.

Simultaneously, the increased use of tax avoidance techniques increases administrative burdens. The Internal Revenue Service in 1983 employed some 85,000 people, about the same number as in 1979. However, during the same period, the number of returns under examination because of tax shelter issues increased from 183,000 to 335,000.[24] As taxpayers devote more resources to avoiding taxes, the tax authorities must either greatly increase expenditures on enforcement or watch the quality of administration decline.

The costs of administration and compliance can be reduced by structural tax reform. Simplification would be promoted by reducing the number of special deductions, credits, and allowances. Moving to a comprehensive personal tax of any kind—on annual income, lifetime income, or consumption—would help achieve this end. But this simplification can come only if Congress is prepared to forbear using the tax system to achieve nonrevenue goals. Such forbearance could be encouraged by the knowledge that beyond a certain point piecemeal incentives tend to become self-defeating. Incentives result from *relative* advantages; if tax

---

23. *Statistics of Income Bulletin*, vol. 3, No. 1 (Summer 1983), p. 45; vol. 4, no. 1 (Summer 1984), forthcoming.

24. Internal Revenue Service, *Annual Report of the Commissioner and Chief Counsel, 1980*, p. 27; *1983*, p. 11.

concessions are pervasive, the relative advantage of favored activities declines.

A more fundamental approach to achieving simplification would be to deal directly with the realization principle underlying the income tax. Under present law, accrual accounting is necessarily imperfectly implemented. Therefore, the taxpayer who can defer the realization of income can also defer taxes. Deferral reduces the burden of those taxes, even if the amount of tax is not diminished, since future payments have a lower present value than do current payments. Even under a comprehensive annual income tax, with capital gains taxed in full, large advantages would accrue to taxpayers who could convert their ordinary income into deferrable capital gains.

Eliminating the advantages of tax deferral would close this avenue for tax avoidance and would forestall the increase in compliance and administrative costs associated with policing such tax-motivated transactions. But, as indicated above, such an approach cannot be taken within the framework of the annual income tax.

Even reforms that promise eventually to simplify administration and compliance may increase complexity in the short run. Large-scale reforms often require transition rules to ease the burdens for those taxpayers who are losing major concessions or to minimize the effects of tax changes on asset prices. These transition rules are almost always complex, but they are necessary to assure equity during the shift to a new set of rules.

What do alternative strategies accomplish?

This section evaluates four strategies of tax reform: a return to principles of personal annual income taxation; adoption of the personal lifetime income tax principle; introduction of a broad-based nonpersonal tax on consumption (the value-added tax); and the expansion of excise taxes to new commodities and an increase in the rate of existing excise taxes, especially alcohol and tobacco. Each of these strategies will be measured against three related criteria. What problems with the present tax system does it solve? What problems with the present system does it leave unsolved? And what problems does it introduce or worsen? In answering these questions, we shall consider each strategy in its pure and therefore least distortionary form. We recognize that if any of these strategies is pursued inconsistently or unwisely, the benefits could be reduced or eliminated and the added problems vastly increased.

Comprehensive Income Taxation

The Bradley-Gephardt bill is the most fully articulated proposal now under discussion to tax annual income comprehensively.[25] In some respects it is still a compromise with pure income tax principles (for example, despite the exclusion of in-kind rental income to homeowners, deductions for mortgage interest are still allowed, although only at the lowest of the three tax rates in the proposed schedule, and the rules used in calculating capital income do not provide for indexing for inflation). Nevertheless, the bill enables one to identify certain problems with the current system that are solved, others that are not solved, and at least one that is made worse.

Problems solved. By including many currently excluded fringe benefits and by narrowing the variations in effective tax rates on capital income from alternative investments, the Bradley-Gephardt proposal would reduce distortions in both worker compensation (or in-kind consumption) and investment. Through these provisions and by terminating the exclusion of 60 percent of long-term capital gains, Bradley-Gephardt would sharply reduce the incentive to set up tax shelters and other efforts to avoid tax. The widened tax base would permit current revenues to be collected at reduced marginal rates, an important result because incentives to avoid tax and the attendant economic distortions increase with the marginal tax rate.

Problems not solved. Certain problems remain under the Bradley-Gephardt proposal and would continue under any annual personal income tax. Most relate to the measurement of capital income each year. Accurate measurement would require the indexation of depreciation, interest income, and capital gains and the inclusion in taxable income of unrealized as well as realized capital gains. The Bradley-Gephardt proposal makes no advance in any of these directions.[26] It continues to rely on unindexed depreciation in calculating investment income; it does not call for indexing the computation of capital gains; it fully taxes nominal interest without

25. S. 1421, Fair Tax Act of 1983. See *Congressional Record,* daily edition (June 8, 1983), pp. S7836–57. For a brief description of this proposal, see the appendix. Other bills introduced in Congress to broaden the tax base and lower rates include S. 1040 by Sen. Dan Quayle, Republican of Indiana, and S. 557 by Sen. Dennis DeConcini, Democrat of Arizona (the latter based on the proposal by Robert E. Hall and Alvin Rabushka in their *Low Tax, Simple Tax, Flat Tax* (McGraw-Hill, 1983).

26. The repeal of tax bracket (or rate) indexing under the Bradley-Gephardt proposal, although undesirable in our judgment, is an incidental feature that has no bearing on the problems with current law that a comprehensive income tax base is capable of solving.

allowance for inflation; and it taxes only realized income. Although practical methods exist to eliminate the inflation-related distortions of depreciation deductions,[27] solutions to the other problems may be impracticable under the income tax.[28]

Problems increased. A return to the principles of annual personal income taxation would aggravate one existing problem, which is the distortion of the choice between consuming income now or saving it for later consumption. The introduction of numerous ways by which individuals may receive capital income without currently paying tax on it (IRAs, Keogh plans, and qualified pension plans, for example) has reduced the degree to which capital income is subject to tax as earned at the personal level. Although these provisions cause capital income to be taxed at widely varying rates and provide many opportunities for tax arbitrage, they have placed many taxpayers (although not most saving) in the position where they can decide between present and future consumption on the basis of rates of return undistorted by the tax system. The increase in taxes on capital income under Bradley-Gephardt would restore this distortion to the decisions of many taxpayers who now are free from it.

The Lifetime Income Tax

The lifetime income tax consists of two elements: an annual personal tax on total cash receipts (including inheritances) less saving (with gifts and bequests classified as consumption); and a corporation tax on cash flow.[29] This tax system solves most of

27. Some distortions caused by inflation could be avoided if investors were permitted to deduct in the first year in which an investment is made the present value of the depreciation deductions to which they would be entitled if there were no inflation. Although such a rule largely insulates depreciation from inflation-related distortions, it does nothing about the distortion of capital gains or of interest income. See Alan J. Auerbach and Dale W. Jorgenson, "Inflation-Proof Depreciation of Assets," *Harvard Business Review,* vol. 58 (September–October 1980), pp. 113–18.

28. See Henry J. Aaron, ed., *Inflation and the Income Tax* (Brookings Institution, 1976).

29. For details of this proposal, see the appendix. In addition, one can consult the following sources: William D. Andrews, "A Consumption-Type or Cash Flow Personal Income Tax," *Harvard Law Review,* vol. 87 (April 1974), pp. 1113–88; Anthony B. Atkinson and Joseph E. Stiglitz, *Lectures on Public Economics* (McGraw-Hill, 1980), especially chap. 3; David F. Bradford, "The Economics of Tax Policy Toward Savings," in George M. von Furstenberg, ed., *The Government and Capital Formation* (Ballinger, 1980), pp. 11–17; David F. Bradford, "Issues in the Design of Savings and Investment Incentives," in Charles R. Hulten, ed., *Depreciation, Inflation, and the Taxation of Income from Capital* (Washington, D.C.: Urban Institute, 1981), pp. 13–47; Hall and Rabushka, *Low Tax, Simple Tax, Flat Tax;* Sven-Olof Lodin, *Progressive Expenditure Tax—An Alternative?* a report of the 1972 Government Commission on Taxation (Stockholm: LiberFörlag, 1978); *The Structure and Reform of Direct Taxation,* report of a committee chaired by J. E. Meade for the Institute for Fiscal Studies (London: George Allen and Unwin, 1978); Peter

the problems with the existing personal and corporation income taxes that were described earlier, but it creates certain new problems, some of which are transitional.

Problems solved. The lifetime income tax, as described in the appendix, accurately measures an individual's capacity to consume over his or her lifetime, whereas the annual income tax does not. A corollary of this proposition is that the lifetime income tax ends the present distortion of the choice between consuming and saving. Like a return to the principles of annual income taxation, it would eliminate distortions in the composition of workers' compensation and in consumption that result from the exclusion of fringe benefits from personal tax.

The lifetime income tax also eliminates a wide range of problems relating to the measurement of capital income. Because investment would be expensed rather than depreciated, the value of these deductions would not be affected by inflation. The decision about when to realize capital income would be unaffected by the tax system because the spendable proceeds would be the same whenever realization occurred.[30] Discrepancies in the effective rate of tax on capital income and attendant distortions of investments would be eliminated.

The combination of a cash flow tax on corporations and a lifetime income tax on individuals would eliminate the problem of integrating the personal and corporation taxes. The corporation tax would fall only on cash flowing to foreign persons and entities not subject to U.S. taxation and on extraordinary rates of return.

The prospects for correctly treating the flow of incomes associated with owner-occupied housing are better under the lifetime income tax than under any income tax. Correct treatment under the income tax requires the taxation of net imputed rent rather than the deduction of mortgage interest and property taxes.[31] Such a change is politically difficult to accomplish since

---

Mieszkowski, "The Advisability and Feasibility of an Expenditure Tax System," in Henry J. Aaron and Michael J. Boskin, eds., *The Economics of Taxation* (Brookings Institution, 1980), pp. 179–201; Joseph A. Pechman, ed., *What Should Be Taxed: Income or Expenditure?* (Brookings Institution, 1980); and U.S. Department of the Treasury, *Blueprints for Basic Tax Reform* (GPO, 1977).

30. This statement assumes that the tax rate is the same in all periods in which realization is considered and rests on the fact that the present value of tax liabilities would be independent of the timing of realization. Clearly, realization would be affected if rates were expected to be different in two periods (for example, because a worker anticipates lower tax rates after he or she retires). Such tax-induced alterations in realization would be desirable, because they would achieve a degree of voluntary averaging.

31. In principle, tax should be levied on net imputed rent, NR, defined as the excess of estimated gross market rent, GR, over mortgage interest, MI, property taxes, PT, and

net imputed rent is an item of income that does not generate a cash flow and one that can be estimated only indirectly. While the political obstacles to equalizing the treatment of owner-occupied housing and other investments under the lifetime income tax would also be formidable, the device for achieving this goal may be more palatable. Although the lifetime income tax would not permit carrying a mortgage at tax-deductible interest rates to earn tax-free imputed rents, it would in general extend to other assets many of the advantages now available only to owner-occupied housing, resulting in equal treatment of housing and other investments.[32]

---

all other expenses including depreciation, OE. In other words $NR = GR - PT - MI - OE$. To reach this result, one could either disallow deductions for PT and MI and include NR in the tax base directly, or calculate NR indirectly by introducing deductions for OE and including GR.

32. As with any other investment, the cost of a house under the lifetime income tax should, in principle, be immediately deductible, and the withdrawals from qualified accounts or the proceeds from loans used to pay for the house should be included in taxable receipts. These transactions would exactly offset one another so that the transactions in combination would not affect current tax. However, future rental income from the house should then be included in the tax base of the owner and repayment of the loan and other investment costs should be deductible. Any difference would be reflected in each future year's tax base.

Unique aspects of owner-occupied housing may make this approach impractical. In particular, the owner receives no cash rent. If a deduction is allowed for the purchase price, exactly offset by the inclusion of proceeds of home mortgages and withdrawals from tax-sheltered accounts for the down payment, and if no rental flow is included in receipts, a deduction for loan repayments would provide owner-occupants a large tax shelter. To avoid this problem, some analysts have suggested excluding all aspects of the purchase of a home from the tax system. That is, no deduction would be given for the investment and neither the proceeds of mortgages nor their repayments would have any effect on tax. Only the amounts withdrawn from tax-sheltered accounts for down payments would be subject to tax.

This approach simplifies the tax treatment of housing but raises other problems. The size of down payments could cause large bulges in consumption and hence in tax. This problem could be solved by averaging; that is, each year for perhaps ten years, a deduction could be allowed that is equal to the amortization of the down payment at the mortgage interest rate.

Alternatively, a house purchase could be treated like any other investment, but owner-occupants could be required to include in each year's tax base a practical approximation of the gross rental stream. The approximation would be based on guideline percentages adjusted for changes in gross rents and applied to the purchase price of the house. This procedure would yield a set of calculated gross rents designed to provide a fair rate of return on the value of the asset. The value of the flows discounted at that rate of return would just equal the initial deduction for the price paid for the house. Under this approach, a deduction would be given for the purchase price, the proceeds of mortgages and funds withdrawn from qualified accounts would be included in current receipts, and loan amortization would be fully deductible. Like the attempt to tax net imputed rent under the annual income tax, this approach suffers from the shortcoming that sizable tax liabilities would hinge on imputations that might err significantly in individual cases.

Problems created or increased. Although the lifetime income tax would eliminate most problems associated with the calculation of capital income, it would increase informational requirements in certain other areas. To calculate the individual tax base, it would be necessary to keep track of all capital flows, including those which are irrelevant under current law because they are not associated with income. Thus, shifts in funds among accounts would have to be reported. The problem under current law of dealing equitably with large variations in income would be replaced by a smaller problem of dealing fairly with variations in consumption.[33]

The lifetime income tax would create certain administrative problems, some of which would be transitional, although they could persist for some time. If nothing else were done, the switch to a lifetime income tax would be unfair to people, such as older workers and retirees, who had accumulated assets out of previously taxed income; without special transition rules, such assets would be taxed a second time when consumed. Note that this problem does not exist with respect to consumption out of current earnings or out of previously untaxed income such as social security benefits,[34] employer-financed pension benefits, individual retirement accounts, and Keogh plans.[35] These sources of income constitute about 74 percent of the income of the elderly.[36]

33. The problem would be smaller for three reasons: consumption varies less from year to year than does income; lumpy outlays would be averaged by formula; and households would be able to make some expenditures from borrowing outside the framework of tax-sheltered accounts.

34. Except to the extent that social security benefits have been financed by employee payroll taxes.

35. At some increase in complexity it would be possible to tax under old law any capital gains that were accrued before the transition to the new system. Such an approach would complicate the transition, and we see no serious loss in fairness if all net reductions in wealth holdings are taxed equally under the new law regardless of when such wealth was amassed, so long as no tax had previously been imposed on the current holder. For a contrary view, see Department of the Treasury, *Blueprints for Basic Tax Reform.* With respect to other previously untaxed income, there is no conceptual issue. For example, taxes have already been paid on the portion of social security benefits that represents the return of employee contributions. Eventually these contributions will represent half of the present value of benefits. Because no one has paid social security taxes over an entire working life sufficient to fund the benefits to be received, the present value of employee payroll taxes for all persons who have retired is much below half of the value of benefits.

36. Melinda Upp, "Relative Importance of Various Income Sources of the Aged, 1980," *Social Security Bulletin,* vol. 46 (January 1983), pp. 3–10. Earnings and retirement pensions (including social security, government employee pensions, and private pensions) account for 74 percent of total income of the entire survey group and 65 percent of total income of units with incomes of $20,000 or more. "Asset income" and "public assistance" are the other income categories.

In dealing with the transition, one faces a trade-off between simplicity and individualized treatment. Stressing simplicity, one might solve the problem for most taxpayers by allowing everyone over particular ages an exemption for some amount of consumption. Stressing individualized treatment, one might allow each household to recover tax free the aggregate cost of all assets accumulated from savings out of previously taxed income.[37] This could be accomplished by allowing deductions against the tax flow cash base spread over a number of years for consumption until that aggregate cost had been deducted in total.

Special transition rules would also be necessary under the corporate cash flow tax to deal with existing capital and debt. Firms should be allowed to write off the undepreciated cost of all capital in existence at the time the new tax rules take effect and be required to take outstanding debt into the tax base.

Also, until such time as states coordinated their annual personal taxes with the new federal system, taxpayers might have to continue certain accounts necessary for calculating their state income tax as well as the new records necessary for the lifetime income tax. A more lasting administrative problem would arise from the increased incentive of taxpayers to conceal capital transactions under a lifetime income tax. Under current law, a taxpayer who conceals a capital transaction may save tax on the gain on such a transaction. Under the proposed system, the taxpayer could save tax on the entire principal of a concealed transaction. The increased incentive to conceal transactions would require heightened administrative efforts to prevent such evasion.

Last, issues of international tax harmonization would have to be resolved under the lifetime income and corporate cash flow taxes, particularly if the rest of the world remains committed to annual income taxation. Among other things, rules would be required for the taxation of income from foreign investment in the United States, from U.S. investment abroad, and for the treatment of immigration and emigration.

We have already noted the desirability of implementing a withholding tax at the business level for payments to foreign investors, but new procedures would be required in other cases. Consistent with the corporation cash flow tax, no deductions from or additions to the tax base would result from dividend and equity flows between the corporation and its foreign subsidiaries. But a separate decision on the creditability of foreign taxes paid

37. This aggregate amount corresponds to "basis" in current tax law.

by the subsidiary would still be required. Alternative approaches are possible, ranging from denial of a credit for foreign taxes paid to a full credit up to some specified rate.[38]

The Value-Added Tax

The value-added tax is a sales tax levied at each stage of production on "value added," which is the difference between total sales proceeds and the cost of goods and services purchased from other firms. The most frequently discussed form of the value-added tax permits firms to deduct immediately the cost of all investments. As a result, a comprehensive value-added tax may be shown to be equivalent to a tax on all consumption. It has the same economic effects as a truly comprehensive retail sales tax.

No country now imposes a comprehensive value-added tax, however, and all of the proposals advanced in the United States would excuse a large share of consumption from the tax. Two factors explain the attraction of partial value-added taxes. The first concerns the distributional effects of a comprehensive value-added tax. Such a tax would be proportional to consumption but regressive with respect to annual income (because the proportion of income that is saved rises with income) and with respect to lifetime income (because it would not reach bequests, which rise more than proportionately with lifetime income). Most countries have sought to reduce this regressivity by excusing from full taxation those goods on which low-income families spend larger-than-average shares of their incomes. This policy has made the value-added tax roughly proportional to annual income in some countries.

Second, a truly comprehensive value-added tax would have to tax such activities as services of financial institutions and nonprofit organizations and either purchases or the imputed rental services of owner-occupied housing and other durable consumer goods. Because the taxation of these activities is very difficult to administer, no existing value-added tax includes them all. Yet, these exclusions create administrative complexities of their own and generate economic inefficiency as resources tend to flow to the

38. Since foreign taxes under current law are creditable against U.S. taxes only up to the U.S. tax rate, a denial of the foreign tax credit is consistent with the view that the effective U.S. rate on marginal investment is zero under the corporation cash flow tax. However, to ease the concerns of foreign governments who might claim that the United States in this way would be making domestic investment more attractive than foreign investment, thereby violating the principle of capital export neutrality, foreign taxes, as a political matter, could be made creditable to some degree against domestic taxes.

more lightly taxed activities. It is impossible to know exactly
how broad the base for a value-added tax would be in the United
States. Most proposals have suggested taxing about half of all
consumption.

Problems solved, not solved. The main problem that a value-
added tax would help solve is an insufficiency of tax revenues. A
value-added tax would raise in net revenues about $13 billion per
percentage point of tax in 1989, depending on the comprehen-
siveness of the tax base.[39] But the value-added tax cannot achieve
a fair, efficient, or simple tax system unless it is combined with
direct reforms of personal and business taxes. The advent of a
value-added tax would do nothing directly to remove the disparate
effective rates of tax on different investments, on saving versus
consumption, or on cash receipts versus fringe benefits. It would
not stop inflation from aggravating these distortions. By permitting a given total revenue to be collected with less reliance on
personal and corporation income taxes, a value-added tax would
reduce somewhat the distortions their flawed tax bases now cause.
But these gains should not be attributed to the value-added tax;
they would accrue equally whatever the revenue source.

Problems created. Among the new problems that a value-added
tax would create, three stand out. The first concerns the distribution of tax burdens. Under the personal income tax, some low-
income earners now actually receive subsidies, because they qualify
for the earned-income tax credit, a payment based on earnings
provided to many persons with earned income below $11,000 per
year (after the Tax Reform Act of 1984). A value-added tax would
subject such families to significant tax liabilities. Other families
who pay little income tax would experience heavier tax burdens
under a value-added tax than under income taxes. It would be
possible to prevent such a shift of burdens to low-income households by providing refundable personal income tax credits or
increased and broadened transfer payments. But these credits
would either require tax returns from millions of low-income
persons who are not now required to file tax returns or bring
millions of new households under some system of transfer payments. The result would be increases in the cost of administering
and complying with tax laws and transfer programs. A value-
added tax, therefore, would create a dilemma of burdening with
taxes people now regarded as too poor to pay them or creating

39. This amount is net of the effect on income tax revenue attributable to the increased
gap between output at market prices and income at factor cost.

additional administrative burdens for such families and for the government.

A second problem concerns the relationship between a value-added tax and the many existing state and local retail sales taxes. In the view of many, a value-added tax would reduce the degree to which state and local governments could continue to rely on retail sales taxes. This problem would be reduced if a value-added tax were imposed at rates sufficiently high to meet federal revenue goals and to provide grants to states in return for which the states would give up retail sales taxation. But it is unlikely that states would willingly surrender the fiscal autonomy that such a swap would require.

The third problem that a value-added tax would create is additional administrative costs for both the government and private businesses. This problem would arise unless the value-added tax proceeds were sufficient to completely replace those of another major tax such as the corporation income tax. But such replacement would mean that the first 6 to 7 percentage points of the value-added tax would serve only to replace existing revenues, not to reduce the federal deficit. The value-added tax would have to be set at about 14 percent to cover the loss of corporate tax revenue and to yield an additional $100 billion for closing the deficit. With such a rate, potentially significant distortions would be introduced between taxed and untaxed consumption. Furthermore, such a rate would greatly aggravate the problem of new tax burdens on low-income households.

Selective Excise Taxes

Recent legislation has increased federal reliance on selective excise taxes. The Tax Equity and Fiscal Responsibility Act of 1982 and the Highway Revenue Act of 1982 together increased excise tax collections by more than $8 billion at fiscal 1984 levels.[40] Excise taxes are projected to raise $38 billion in fiscal 1984: $23 billion from taxes on alcohol, tobacco, telephone services, the windfall profit tax, and miscellaneous excises; and $15 billion from highway excises (primarily gasoline taxes) and airport and airway excises.[41]

For excises to play a major revenue-raising role, however, their

40. This estimate is net of income tax offsets. The excise tax increases on tobacco and telephone services enacted in the 1982 bill were only temporary through September 30, 1985. In the Tax Reform Act of 1984, Congress allowed the tobacco tax increase to lapse but extended the telephone tax until 1987 and increased excise taxes on distilled spirits.

41. *The Budget of the United States Government, FY 1985*, pp. 9-19–9-20.

application would have to be expanded considerably; energy consumption has been considered a likely new source of excise tax revenue. The revenue potential of a broad-based tax on the use of all forms of energy is substantial—about $4 billion at fiscal 1989 levels for each 1 percent tax on value.[42] Aside from the political difficulties of implementing such a tax, this approach to raising revenues poses many of the same issues as the value-added tax.

Problems solved, not solved. Excise taxes could help lower the deficit, but they could not yield enough revenue to close it. Some selective excises, the so-called "sin taxes" on alcohol and tobacco, might reduce the incidence of certain diseases and of traffic injuries and fatalities. But these and other selective excise taxes would neither correct the shortcomings of the personal and corporation income taxes nor spare the nation the need to raise additional revenues from broad-based taxes.

Problems created. Particular excise taxes, by definition, apply to only a few goods. They are likely, therefore, to interfere more with consumer choices than do broad-based taxes. Because tastes for a narrow set of goods vary greatly among households, selective excises are likely to violate the fundamental precept that equals should be taxed equally. Furthermore, the heavy use of such excises as gasoline or other energy taxes would increase the degree to which federal and state governments are using the same tax bases.

Other than the argument that heavy energy use imposes general costs not expressed in the market price (such as the alleged damage to the United States from greater dependence on foreign energy sources), no strong case can be made for a greater use of energy excise taxes.

Conclusion

Tax revenues must be increased and the tax system must be reformed to improve its equity and to reduce tax-related distortions of economic decisions. The tax system should be simplified both to reduce costs of compliance and enforcement and to enable taxpayers to understand the system through which they pay for public services.

Our current income tax system has gone astray, in large measure because it has ceased to reflect any coherent unifying principle. The income tax at all times has suffered from shortcomings inherent in the way it treats capital income. But the mélange of

42. Congressional Budget Office, *Reducing the Deficit: Spending and Revenue Options* (CBO, February 1984), p. 228.

inconsistent principles in various aspects of the income tax has produced absurd complexity and unintended and indefensible distortions. Major improvements in fairness, efficiency, and administrative ease will occur only if reforms reflect a consistent set of principles.

Appendix   *The Bradley-Gephardt Proposal*

The Fair Tax Act of 1983 (S. 1421), sponsored by Senator Bill Bradley, Democrat of New Jersey, and Representative Richard Gephardt, Democrat of Missouri, would eliminate the 60 percent exclusion for long-term capital gains, reduce depreciation allowances or eliminate the investment credit for depreciable capital, include unemployment compensation in the tax base, repeal deductions for state and local taxes other than income and property taxes, and end the exclusion of certain fringe benefits including employer-purchased health insurance.[43] These and other measures to broaden the tax base would permit the same revenues to be collected as under current law with three rate brackets of 14, 26, and 30 percent. Personal exemptions would be set at $1,600 per taxpayer. In addition there would be a zero-bracket amount of $3,000 for single persons and $6,000 for others. Only the 14 percent rate would be applied to income earned by pension funds. Personal exemptions and itemized deductions would apply only against the 14 percent rate; in other words, the extra tax above 14 percent would fall on income gross of these deductions. The Bradley-Gephardt bill would repeal rate indexing.

About 80 percent of all taxpayers would be subject to the bottom rate of 14 percent. For joint returns, the 14 percent rate would apply to the first $40,000 of taxable income; the 26 percent rate would apply to the next $25,000; and the 30 percent rate would apply to taxable income exceeding $65,000. These rates would apply to the following income brackets for single returns: up to $25,000; $25,000 to $37,500; and exceeding $37,500.

At the corporate level, the proposal would repeal the investment tax credit and make several other changes that would broaden the tax base. Again, a reduction of the tax rate from the current level of 46 percent to 30 percent, which would be the same as the top-

43. Bill Bradley, *The Fair Tax* (Pocket Books, 1984). For general analyses of comprehensive income tax proposals, see Joseph A. Minarik, "The Future of the Individual Income Tax," *National Tax Journal,* vol. 35 (September 1982), pp. 236–41; and Joseph A. Pechman and John Karl Scholtz, "Comprehensive Income Taxation and Rate Reduction," *Tax Notes,* vol. 17 (October 11, 1982), pp. 83–93 (Brookings Reprint 390).

bracket rate applicable to individuals, would offset the revenue effects of base broadening.

The Lifetime Income Tax

The base of a lifetime income tax would be comprehensive receipts less saving. The tax on saving would be deferred until the savings were consumed or transferred to others by gift or bequest. The proceeds of consumption loans would be included in the tax base. Also, end-of-lifetime wealth representing unexercised potential consumption of the taxpayer would be included in the tax base.

Receipts would include all wages and salaries, rent, interest, profits, dividends, transfer payments, gifts received, and inheritances. Savings would be defined as all payments into certain "qualified accounts," including all financial assets (stocks, bonds, and other securities), all accounts in banks and other depository institutions, and purchases of real estate (except owner-occupied housing).[44]

Just as additions to savings are deducted from income, withdrawals from qualified accounts (or dissaving) would be added to the tax base. Similarly, the proceeds of loans would be included in the tax base, and loan repayments, including both principal and interest, would be deductable in calculating the tax base.

Inheritances and gifts received would be counted as a receipt, but if they were not consumed, they would be exactly offset by an increase in savings. Gifts and bequests made would be treated as consumption in the year during which they occur, subject to an averaging provision if the amounts transferred were large relative to annual income.

It would be desirable to award each person a lifetime exemption for a certain amount of gifts or bequests to permit tax-free transfers, for example between parents or children at time of need. But very large exemptions would result in unequal taxes on people with similar lifetime spending capacities. A lifetime exemption of $100,000 per person ($200,000 per couple) would permit most families to exclude all gifts and bequests from tax. But since most wealth transferred between generations is concen-

---

44. Accrued gains of all kinds would not be taxable until realized and then only if not saved. Thus, accrued gains would be ignored in practice; in principle, they may be regarded as adding equally to income and saving and hence offsetting one another.

trated in large estates, such an exemption would not materially erode the principle that lifetime income should be taxed in full.[45]

Personal exemptions allowed under the current income tax system would be continued, although the exact amount should be modified. We propose as a minimum standard that no tax be imposed on persons whose consumption equals current poverty thresholds.[46] Based on estimates for 1984, tax-free levels of consumption would be set at $5,000 for a single person, $8,250 for couples, and $1,500 for each additional dependent. In addition, some account should be taken of the fact that one-earner families are better off than two-earner families with the same income. Two-earner families lose in-home services provided by the non-earning spouse in a one-earner household and may incur money costs for child care and other household services. Accordingly, we recommend continuing the current deduction of 10 percent of the earnings of the spouse with lesser earnings up to some maximum earnings level ($30,000 per year under current law).[47] Similarly, a credit for low earners, like the earned-income tax credit now allowed certain workers with low earnings, might also be provided.

Tax rates would be progressive under the lifetime income tax to approximate the current distribution of tax burdens. For joint returns, annual consumption would be taxed as follows: 5 percent on the first $10,000 of taxable expenditures; 20 percent on the next $30,000; and 32 percent on taxable expenditures exceeding $40,000 per year. For single taxpayers, the same rates would apply to taxable expenditure brackets of less than $5,000; $5,000 to $40,000; and more than $40,000.

Personal deductions or credits other than those already noted would be severely limited. For defining ability to pay, deductions

45. Widows and widowers would inherit the exemption of their deceased spouse, but no person would be allowed more than a $200,000 exemption, even if successive spouses have died. The calculation of the value of wealth transfers included in the tax base was based on a methodology developed by Daphne Greenwood in "An Estimation of U.S. Family Wealth and its Distribution from Microdata, 1973," *Review of Income and Wealth,* vol. 29 (March 1983), pp. 23–44. For an excellent discussion of estate tax avoidance, see George Cooper, *A Voluntary Tax? New Perspectives on Sophisticated Estate Tax Avoidance* (Brookings Institution, 1979). Effective implementation of the cash flow tax would require a major reduction in the opportunities for avoiding tax on wealth transfers.

46. We recognize that the consistency of the official thresholds has been subject to some criticism and that the relative level of the thresholds for families of different sizes may require revision. For that reason the exact numbers are illustrative only. Some variation in the level of exemptions for families of different sizes might well be desirable.

47. This credit would have the effect of increasing tax-free levels of consumption for two-earner families.

could be allowed for extraordinary medical expenses or for casualty losses on assets that have not been expensed. As a matter of social policy, a tax credit (equal to the top marginal rate) could be provided for charitable contributions.

The corporation tax would consist of two parts. The first would be a tax on cash flow. The corporation tax base would include total receipts of the corporation from all sources other than the sale of stock, less all business expenses, including investment in the year paid for.[48] Deductions for business expenditures on consumption items for the benefit of employees or owners would be denied.[49] The business tax base would include the proceeds from borrowing. Corporations would be entitled to deduct all debt service payments, but no deductions would be permitted for dividends or any other cash distribution to stockholders. If firms borrowed to finance investment, no tax would result in the year the investment was made; the expenditure on the investment would just offset the proceeds from the loan. If earnings on the investment differed from the repayment of debt, corporate cash flow and tax liabilities would be affected.[50]

The second element of the tax on corporations would be a withholding tax on all distributions from corporations to both individuals and other corporations not subject to U.S. taxation. This tax would apply to dividends, interest, rents, royalties, and any other cash distribution. Exemptions from such withholding would be granted for payments into qualified accounts of U.S. taxpayers. But this withholding tax would be final for taxpayers not subject to U.S. taxation.

The expensing of new corporate investment under the cash

48. Immediate deduction of the cost of investments would generate tax losses for new firms or for firms otherwise earning small profits. For deductibility to be as valuable on investments undertaken by such firms as it would be for profitable firms, a variety of steps could be undertaken. Firms could be allowed to carry tax losses forward to be applied against future cash flow. If this course is followed, the losses should be accumulated with interest to assure that their present value does not decline over time, a potentially serious problem when interest rates are high. In addition, firms could be allowed to offset any current negative cash flow against previous positive cash flow and receive rebates of previous taxes paid, similar to tax-loss carrybacks allowed under current law. In principle, past taxes should also be increased by the discount factor, but so long as interest is paid on loss carryforwards, this additional refinement is of limited significance.

49. Deductions for consumption expenditures by noncorporate businesses would also be denied.

50. The same principles would be applied to cash flow of noncorporate businesses. In particular, new investments and debt transactions would be treated in the same way. Net cash flow, however, would be included immediately in the tax base of the owners, although there would be an offsetting deduction for saving if the funds remained in the business or were saved.

flow tax, in effect, makes the government a participant in returns that differ from the government's borrowing rate. The business tax deduction for investments at the time of purchase causes an initial reduction of government revenues. The government recovers this "investment" by collecting tax on the return to the investment. The government comes out even when the flow of such taxes, discounted at the government's borrowing rate, just equals the loss of revenue from the initial deduction. The tax has a positive present value to the extent that the business rate of return exceeds the government's borrowing rate. Some part of the return above the government's borrowing rate represents compensation to investors for the riskiness of some corporate investments; but part may represent the extra return to firms that enjoy particularly favorable market positions. Taxation of "rents" on these monopolistic advantages is an improvement in the efficiency of a tax system.

Comment by Charles E. McLure, Jr.

THE DISCUSSANTS' task is never easy, particularly when the assignment involves papers that say as much that is right and as little that is wrong as do the ones by Gordon Henderson and by Henry Aaron and Harvey Galper. Rather than comment point by point on the two papers, I would like to indicate briefly why I think fundamental tax reform is necessary and then go on to more detailed comments.

Need for reform

The income tax system has become exceedingly complex. To some extent this is unavoidable in a tax system that attempts to measure income in a sophisticated economy, draw distinctions between various sources and uses of income, and take account of the personal circumstances of taxpayers. For example, such problems as differentiation between capital gains and ordinary income and between interest and dividends are inherent in a tax system that treats such income flows differently. Similarly, if the taxpaying unit changes because of marriage, divorce, or death, income averaging and rollover of capital gains on a principal residence are inherently difficult in a tax system that allows splitting of income within a family unit and levies taxes annually. For these reasons and others, I cannot agree fully with Henderson's statement that "complexity . . . is not an inherent characteristic of the income tax." And yet, there is much truth to the thrust of his argument: much of the complexity of the present income tax is not inherent; it results in large part from the attempt to use the income tax for a variety of social purposes, rather than as simply a means of raising revenue based on ability to pay. As part of our study of fundamental tax reform, we at the Treasury Department will be examining many exclusions, exemptions, deductions, and credits in the income tax to determine which can be eliminated or at least simplified.

The second basic reason for fundamental tax reform is that the tax system is unfair and is perceived to be unfair; to some extent the perception is founded in reality. Through either legal or illegal means some taxpayers are paying far less income tax than they should. This problem can be relieved through improved administration and new enforcement techniques such as concentrated efforts to attack abusive tax shelters. But some aspects of the problem can probably be addressed satisfactorily only through fundamental tax reform that will increase the fairness of the tax system. The existence of tax shelters, even if they are perfectly legal and were anticipated in legislative history, probably undermines the public's perception of the fairness of the tax system. The result is almost certainly a deterioration in taxpayer morale, of which this country was for so long justly proud, and in taxpayer compliance. When the view becomes widespread that the tax system is unfair and that others are not paying their share, a system based on voluntary compliance is likely to crumble, and no degree of improved administration can save it, short of a virtual police state.

The third reason that fundamental tax reform is needed, though one that may appeal more to economists than to others, is the lack of neutrality of the existing system. Twenty years ago, following the lead of Al Harberger, economists were emphasizing the sectoral distortions inherent in the separate, unintegrated taxation of corporate equity income. Now this analysis has been superseded by Mervyn A. King's and Don Fullerton's *Taxation of Income from Capital* (University of Chicago Press, 1984). The book presents an eighty-one cell analysis of tax-induced distortions based on three types of assets, three broad industrial groups, three sources of finance, and three types of owners of assets. And this is only for the nonfinancial sector! Moreover, it does not fully include the pernicious effects of inflation in distorting the measurement of real income and therefore tax burdens. In addition to these basic distortions produced by the structure of business taxation, our tax system also interferes in important ways with how individuals are compensated and the uses they make of their incomes. An important purpose of fundamental tax reform should be the reduction of all types of distortions.

Desire for low flat rates

Virtually all serious observers of the American tax system agree that fundamental tax reform should involve broadening the base and lowering the rates. Even the relatively unsophisticated must realize that it is better, in principle, to tax all income at a rate of 30 percent than to tax 60 percent of income at a rate of 50 percent. Work effort, saving and investment, and invention and innovative activity would all be greater.

Moreover, it appears that many taxpayers think that the rate structure should be relatively flat. This may come as a disquieting surprise to staunch advocates of progressive rates. But it should be recalled that throughout the early postwar period, the U.S. individual income tax was essentially a flat rate tax, with personal exemptions that rendered roughly 20 percent of tax returns nontaxable. Graduated rates were an important reality for only about 10 percent of those who filed returns. Of course, for that 10 percent the steep graduation of rates applied to taxable income was very real indeed. With essentially flat rates, problems that are inherent in graduated rates, among them income averaging and the tax treatment of second earners, were relatively unimportant for most of the population.

Since the mid-1960s, inflation and bracket creep have made graduated rates a reality for an increasing fraction of the population, and by 1979 progressive rates applied to virtually the entire range of incomes subject to tax. By then roughly a third of low-income tax returns were subject to marginal rates below those prevailing at the same point in the distribution of tax returns in 1961. By comparison, almost half of tax returns showed marginal tax rates higher, in some cases substantially higher, than paid by their counterparts in 1961, even under the much more progressive rate structure prevailing earlier. The across-the-board rate reductions in the Economic Recovery Tax Act of 1981 lowered rates, but it did not substantially affect the ubiquity of progressivity.

The shift in focus

My impression is that many of those who are discussing tax reform today have a focus somewhat different from that characterizing previous discussions. First, there is more concern for neutrality toward saving than characterized previous discussions. Second, tax administration and compliance is now being given equal billing with equity and neutrality as criteria against which to judge tax reform. Third, there is much more concern with transition than before. All of these concerns are, I think, healthy. Unfortunately, dealing with them does not make the tax reformer's job any easier.

I often have the feeling that in tax policy, as in so many other areas, our problems can be traced to someone saying, "Wouldn't it be a good idea if. . .?" Whenever such a question elicits adequate agreement, the law is changed without adequate regard for whether the provision under discussion can be administered satisfactorily or will unacceptably complicate the tax code, the task of the Internal Revenue Service, and the lives of taxpayers. There seems to be growing recognition that rough justice based on a much simpler tax law is much to be desired.

Responsible advocates of tax reform must ask not only what would be the best achievable system if we were beginning in 1913, but what is the best achievable system given seven decades of history. Billions of dollars of investments could be affected by tax reform, producing enormous windfall gains and losses, and occupational and other decisions made by generations of taxpayers cannot lightly be disregarded. Henderson writes of "expectations" and Aaron and Galper of "wrenching decisions," and both stress the need for grandfathering or other transition rules. Besides questions of equity that would bother anyone, there are political questions; will those who are injured—or their lobbyists—stand still for fundamental reforms, especially if reform occurs suddenly? Of course, transition rules work against simplification. My impression is that such disruptions and the need for transition rules are greater under a shift to a tax on consumed income than under less extreme reforms, but that question deserves further study. Moreover, if care is not taken, taxpayers can rearrange their portfolios and economic activities in such a way that the intent of tax reform can be avoided, at least during the transition period. The most obvious example of this under the shift to a cash flow tax would be prereform hoarding (either as cash under the mattress or as deposits abroad) that could be fed back into the system to give the postreform appearance of positive saving.

A concern for increased saving drives much of the impetus for a tax on consumed income or an indirect tax such as a federal value-added tax or retail sales tax. In less extreme options for reform it gives rise to proposals for preferential treatment of certain kinds of savings and investment or the returns therefrom. The trouble with piecemeal approaches to this problem, including most attempts to reach a consumption-based direct tax by attrition, is that preferential treatment of saving is not ordinarily accompanied by restrictions on the deductibility of interest or on the use to which borrowed funds can be put. As Aaron and Galper indicate, taxpayers can simply shift assets from taxable investments into tax-preferred investments; this allows them to reduce taxes without increasing net saving. Of course, the extent to which this can be done is limited, at least for most taxpayers, by the modest amount of financial assets they hold. In more extreme cases, taxpayers can take advantage of inconsistencies in the tax law to engage in arbitrage, by borrowing and paying tax-deductible interest in order to make investments that are tax deductible, that yield tax-preferred returns, or both. The problem, then, is to devise a system that provides preferential treatment of saving without opening avenues for wholesale tax arbitrage. This problem is, of course, accentuated by inflation. An important advantage of a pure cash flow consumption tax is that it handles this arbitrage problem automatically.

Value-added tax   Despite its generally positive contribution, I found Henderson's discussion of the value-added tax to contain a number of statements that were questionable and several that appear to be wrong. To some extent this merely confirms the theory of comparative advantage, since most of the problems involve questionable economic analysis. Given the potential importance of the issues at stake, I think it worthwhile to express my reservations. First, Henderson says, "If an accretion tax discriminates against saving in relation to consumption, then it must follow (since this is its goal) that a consumption tax would do the opposite, that is, discriminate against consumption in relation to saving. But if American individuals were to reduce their consumption expenditures, this would most surely hurt the economy. . . . The decline in consumption could create economic disruption, which in turn could lead to short-term stimulative fiscal policies, greater deficits, and greater inflationary pressure." This passage contains at least two questionable propositions. First, it is important to realize that a consumption tax is (under certain circumstances) neutral between present and future consumption. By comparison, an income tax penalizes saving for future consumption. That consumption would be lower under the consumption tax than under an income tax is not the same as saying that a consumption tax discriminates against consumption. It is important to get the benchmark of neutrality right.

Second, Henderson is not clear what damage to the economy

he has in mind. Presumably, it is a shortfall in aggregate demand generated by a reduction in consumption not matched by an increase in investment. As Henderson notes, the prospect of imposition of a value-added tax could induce consumers to postpone purchase of major durable goods. I doubt that most economists would feel that reduced aggregate demand is likely to be a major problem over the next few years, given the size of projected budget deficits, or that a drop in consumption would lead to short-term stimulative fiscal policies.

Henderson appears to believe that the value-added tax inevitably has a broader base than a retail sales tax. I do not understand this, for there is no inherent reason that the coverage of retail sales taxes and value-added taxes cannot be approximately the same, and state tax practice under the retail sales tax is not dispositive. Certainly, services can be covered by one as easily as the other. One of the primary advantages of a value-added tax is that investment goods are automatically treated properly under a value-added tax, whereas under a retail sales tax either certain classes of goods must be exempt or businesses must be allowed to buy them tax free if the same goal is to be achieved. But the difference in the difficulty of dealing with dual-use goods, such as cars and a typewriter that can be used either in a business or at home, is not as great as Henderson suggests; in either event fraud is involved. Under the value-added tax the purchaser must lie to the tax administrator, while under the retail sales tax he need lie only to the seller.

Henderson's suggestion that rates must be very high for the value-added tax to generate a significant amount of revenue is surprising. The ability to produce $10–15 billion in revenue per percentage point of tax rate belies this impression, and most observers have felt that the ability of the value-added tax to generate significant amounts of revenue with fairly low rates is one of its most important features. (Indeed, Henderson states later that "the value-added tax would add a powerful new source of revenue for the federal government.")

One difference between a value-added tax and a retail sales tax that I have often emphasized is the fact that the latter could more easily be piggybacked by the states than could the former. The importance of this consideration should not be overemphasized, given the states' general reluctance to utilize federal tax collection capabilities already available to them. Moreover, there is not really very much difference between piggybacking a uniform-rate state retail sales tax on the federal tax and making federal grants of value-added tax revenues to states based on the destination of retail sales, a possibility mentioned by Aaron and Galper.

Other issues

The discussion of the corporate income tax in both papers is rather puzzling. First, neither paper alludes to the proposal of the American Law Institute to allow corporations a deduction for dividends attributable only to new shares. Such an approach avoids the windfall gains inherent in relief from double taxation of all dividends and involves a much smaller loss of federal revenue; it is therefore much more efficient in responding to the basic objection against the separate, unintegrated corporate income tax than is complete dividend relief.

Aaron and Galper's off-handed reference to replacing the corporate income tax with a value-added tax is rather disconcerting. A charitable interpretation would be that they really meant some form of integration, not outright elimination. But presumably they meant exactly what they said, since they were speaking of administrative savings that would not be realized unless the corporate tax were actually eliminated.

As a long-time resident of Texas and a current expatriate resident of California, I am acutely aware of regional differences inherent in various approaches to tax reform. Limiting the deduction for state income taxes would benefit residents of states not now using that tax, in relative terms. Limiting the mortgage deduction would hit California and other high-cost areas especially hard. Restrictions on industrial development bonds would have a particularly heavy impact in states using that source of finance. And so it goes. If all regional differences must be respected, the room for fundamental reform may be limited, indeed.

Fundamental reform is possible

Finally, I would like to take exception to Henderson's view, which Senator Gorton, Richard Goode, and Michael Graetz appear to share, that fundamental tax reform is impossible and that "it might be better to work for more gradual, evolutionary changes in our income tax designed to broaden the base and improve the incentives for saving." I share Henderson's skepticism about whether Congress will enact or maintain a simpler and more comprehensive income tax base. But I have even greater concern about our ability to improve the income tax gradually. If we take on each special interest group separately, our efforts in tax reform will almost certainly fail. In my view, and it appears to be Congressman Gephardt's view as well, the best hope for appreciable improvement in taxation is through fundamental tax reform in order to pit the general interest in a broader base and lower rates directly against all special interests simultaneously. Of course, this does not mean all changes must be introduced simultaneously and suddenly; they could be legislated as a package but introduced in stages.

Comment by Daniel Halperin

I CONTINUE to believe that a broad-based progressive tax on income should be the long-range goal. It is decidedly preferable to a similar tax based in consumption.

I obviously agree with Henry Aaron and Harvey Galper that there are serious problems with the current income tax—they may even be correct that some of these problems are insoluble. But before we opt for an alternative, it is essential to consider several issues:

1. To what extent is the complexity and lack of neutrality of today's tax system inherent in an income tax, as opposed to a reaction to political or other pressures for more favorable treatment of income from certain sources? If the latter is the governing cause, as I believe it most often is, should we not assume, in the absence of compelling evidence to the contrary, that these distinctions will continue under a consumption tax?

2. Is it equitable to completely exempt income from capital from tax? If one does not agree with Aaron and Galper's claims for a consumption tax on equity grounds, as I do not, there are serious trade-offs which require a strong showing that the supposed gains in simplicity and efficiency are significant.

3. Will a consumption tax be simpler for the average taxpayer? I believe not, owing to the additional complexity of dealing with investment, liquidation of investments, and borrowing.

4. Will it be just as difficult to accomplish the transition to a broad-based income tax as to a consumption tax? While there are difficulties with both, I believe the transition to a consumption tax presents problems of a different order of magnitude, which again should and probably will prevent its adoption in the absence of an overwhelming case in its favor.

In light of these beliefs, I deplore the energy that is being devoted to the development of various forms of consumption taxation and the time devoted to its examination. The goal I believe I share with Aaron and Galper—a fairer, simpler, and more efficient tax system—would be better served if we would concentrate on improving the income tax. In particular, we need to examine more carefully the fundamental difficulties of measuring income from capital, properly emphasized by Aaron and Galper, before we conclude that the problems are so serious that we should stop trying.

Equal treatment of spenders and savers

Because in effect it does not tax income from capital, a consumption tax is said to be neutral between current and deferred spending. An income tax, on the other hand, is said to provide a smaller premium for deferred spending than would be expected if there were no tax at all. Thus, some claim an income tax is objectionable on grounds of efficiency—it discourages saving—as well as equity. Aaron and Galper think only the latter is important. If they are correct, then the comparative treatment of spenders and savers becomes, I believe, largely irrelevant to the income versus consumption tax debate.

It may be that if both taxes raised an equal amount of revenue, one could expect some additional saving under a consumption tax. It seems clear, however, that the case has not been made that the magnitude of change would be significant enough to justify a switch to a consumption base, even if one otherwise favored an income tax. I agree with Aaron and Galper that if there were a consensus that national savings should increase, it would be far more direct and effective to take steps to reduce the deficit.

But Aaron and Galper prefer a consumption tax on equity grounds. They believe that equity demands equal burdens (in present value terms) on two individuals who have the same endowment or lifetime consumption potential, regardless of their taste for current versus future consumption. I do not believe this argument stands up as a matter of theory. Perhaps more important, it carries no political weight.

It seems to me that their equity claim cannot be objectively measured. It is a matter of taste. One can as readily believe that an income tax based on ability to pay is fairest and that those who save and build up their capital have a greater capacity to pay tax.

Furthermore, congressional concern rests entirely on the potential impact on saving. If there were agreement that there were better ways to increase saving, the worry would vanish.

Investment neutrality

Aaron and Galper argue that we cannot effectively measure income from capital without enormous complexity. An income tax, despite such complexity, will never be neutral and inevitably will seriously distort investment. Therefore, it would be better, on grounds of both efficiency and simplicity, not to try to tax income from capital.

We need to examine very closely how much of the present disparity is explainable by difficulties of measurement, which we could expect to eliminate if we went to a consumption type of tax, and how much is due to political and other pressures for a preference which will continue despite a zero rate on investment income. In other words, which investments will command a direct subsidy or a negative tax if a consumption tax is adopted?

I think one has to recognize that we are likely to have a large amount of distortion in any circumstance. For instance, it is very hard to believe that the preference for saving in the form of qualified pension plans will not continue in some way; this is particularly so if the consensus were that, in the absence of a tax preference for nondiscriminatory plans, retirement saving would be more concentrated among those with higher incomes, while the rank and file would be left with inadequate protection.

Another area is state and local debt. State officials are now pushing hard to protect industrial development bonds, which most observers would agree do not help government. I do not believe equal interest costs for states and corporations will prove acceptable. It may also be impossible to eliminate the existing preferences for real estate or oil exploration.

Housing is another case. Most consumption tax proponents would change the treatment of home ownership only by denying a deduction for mortgage interest and property taxes. This seems unlikely to happen.

Further, an income tax is said to be almost certain to favor housing because of the difficulty of including the imputed income from home ownership in the base. Yet such imputed income should be as much a part of a consumption tax base as it is a part of an income tax base. Consumption tax advocates do not attempt to tax imputed income directly but rather reach it indirectly through inclusion in the tax base of the down payment and amortization on the mortgage. But, if this is a means of taxing imputed income, it can at least in theory be applied to an income tax as well. I do not mean to suggest this is a likely result but just that the technical difficulties of measuring income are not always the only obstacle and perhaps not even the most important barrier to a broad base.

Aaron and Galper have, however, identified a number of areas where, to achieve neutrality, more than political will is needed.

It will be necessary to solve some fairly serious technical problems and to determine whether it can be done with an acceptable degree of complexity.

The principal issues—unrealized gains, corporate integration, inflation, and the proper treatment of the interest deduction—are important to achieving neutrality under an income tax. But I do not agree that it is time for surrender. I think progress on these questions is possible or at least we have not yet proved that it is not. We certainly should not opt for a consumption tax without first engaging in a serious effort to determine the possibilities of reducing the distortion under an income tax.

As Michael Graetz noted, we have moved toward recognition of unrealized gains in the treatment of straddles. The tax system cannot tolerate a taxpayer's ability to create large tax losses by an investment that will produce an offsetting unrealized gain of approximately the same magnitude. Legislation in 1981 and 1984 has stopped the most obvious maneuvers along these lines, but tax advisers will continue to develop more inventive routes to the same end. I think this will eventually force us to consider taxation of accrued but unrealized gains or at least an offset of realized losses by the amount of such increase in value.

Some say this will create a nation of appraisers, but I think it is quite clear that the tax system would be immensely simpler if the increase in value of holdings were subject to current tax. Most discussions of the issue have ignored these substantial simplifications. I think, therefore, taxation of unrealized gains is more a matter of political will and, to some extent, of finding a way to deal with potential claims of lack of liquidity than it is a question of complexity.

This would be particularly true if it were possible to limit taxation of unrealized gains to assets that are relatively easy to value—for example, securities other than those of closely held corporations and real estate—without creating significant distortion. This is a question that as far as I know has not been seriously considered.

Corporate integration, on the other hand, has been extensively studied. The proposals developed by the Treasury in the Carter administration closely parallel the systems now in force in Europe. Adoption is a political, not a technical, issue. If integration is not possible with an income tax, there is no reason to assume the distortive effect, if any, of a separate corporate tax would not continue in a consumption tax system.

Interest deduction

The present system has been described as neither a consumption tax nor an income tax but a hybrid. An income tax that covers investment income would allow a deduction for interest. Since income is in effect not taxed under a consumption tax, interest is effectively not deductible. The hybrid system creates the possibility of combining an interest deduction with tax-exempt income, which is said to lead to tax arbitrage. It is generally suggested that if borrowing is for the purpose of investing in assets from which the income is not taxed, the interest should not be deductible.

I believe the issue is more complex. For example, we would not deny a government subsidy to a farmer who is highly leveraged. We would not be disturbed even if the farmer's income, without including the subsidy, were less than his borrowing costs. If the purpose of the tax benefit is, like the direct subsidy, to encourage investment in a particular industry, it seems reasonable to allow an interest deduction even though the income is exempt. If income is not taxed, however, because we do not feel able to reach unrealized gains or in order to encourage saving for a particular purpose such as retirement, as opposed to investment in a specific industry, the considerations may be different.

Some would support the investment credit and accelerated depreciation as a necessary offset to the double tax on corporate earnings. If so, it is conceivable that it should be denied to investments made with debt capital.

These are difficult questions which have received insufficient attention from academicians. In the absence of such study I am not yet ready to conclude that we cannot develop sensible rules for handling interest under an income tax.

Simplification

A good deal of the current complexity arises from efforts to control tax shelters, which are sometimes said not to be a concern under a consumption tax. Some writers have suggested otherwise. I have a lot of faith in the legal profession; I am sure they will come up with something. So I think we will find problems that we do not think of today.

In any event, for the ordinary wage earner with a few dollars of investment, the consumption tax appears to me more complicated than an income tax that taxes wages when earned. Savings, borrowing, and dissaving are for the most part irrelevant today, except for the need to determine gain. Michael Graetz points out that withholding is less likely to match liability for tax because if you save, the tax base will be smaller than wages; or if you dissave, your tax base will be larger than wages. This is going to cause complexity which we do not have today.

In addition, if a withdrawal from the stock market or a savings account to buy a house creates taxable income, we are almost certainly going to develop some means to deal with bunching of income. Again that leads to complexity which does not exist today.

In sum, for the little guy the consumption tax promises to be more complicated than the income tax.

Transition

Transition is a serious problem. Admittedly, it would be a problem with any change of great magnitude, but the change to a consumption tax would be especially difficult. Part of the risk involved in a tax-favored investment has to be whether the tax treatment will change, or as Michael Graetz pointed out earlier, whether rates will be reduced, which will reduce the value of the preference that presumably is built in to the pretax return on the investment. People have been talking about broad-based reforms for years. It is not a surprise. It is just part of the risk you take when you invest.

Equity concerns are significantly different if the change is to a consumption tax. Consider an individual with $10,000 in the bank—all after-tax income, wages plus interest. Can we really tax this amount again, under the consumption tax, when it is spent? I think this is an equity problem of a different magnitude.

Conclusion

For all these reasons, I think we ought to concentrate our efforts on doing what we can to improve the income tax system and not explore the unknown of consumption taxation, which to my way of thinking is not a promising change.

Conference Participants

with their affiliations at the time of the conference

Henry J. Aaron *Brookings Institution*

Byrle M. Abbin *Arthur Andersen & Company*

Alan Auerbach *University of Pennsylvania*

Harrison M. Bains, Jr. *Nabisco Brands*

J. Gregory Ballentine *Office of Management and Budget*

David F. Bradford *Princeton University*

Gerard M. Brannon *American Council of Life Insurance*

Ernest S. Christian, Jr. *Patton, Boggs & Blow*

Edwin S. Cohen *Covington & Burling*

Sheldon S. Cohen *Cohen & Uretz*

Steven Cohen *Georgetown University Law Center*

Joseph J. Cordes *George Washington University*

Bruce F. Davie *House Committee on Ways and Means*

Al Davis *House Committee on the Budget*

Gina Despres *Office of Senator Bill Bradley*

Graham P. Dozier III *Wachovia Corporation*

Ralph D. Ebbott *3M*

Raymond Einhorn *American University*

Jonathan B. Forman *Office of Senator Daniel P. Moynihan*

A. Lee Fritschler *Brookings Institution*

Harvey Galper *Brookings Institution*

Richard A. Gephardt *U.S. House of Representatives*

A. E. Germain *Aluminum Company of America*

Richard Goode *Brookings Institution*

Slade Gorton *U.S. Senate*

Michael J. Graetz *Yale University*

John A. Hagan *R. J. Reynolds Industries*

Daniel Halperin *Georgetown University Law Center*

Cyrus J. Halpern *American Telephone & Telegraph*

Jerry A. Hausman *Massachusetts Institute of Technology*

Roger L. Headrick *Pillsbury Company*

Gordon D. Henderson *Weil, Gotshal & Manges*

Frederic W. Hickman *Hopkins & Sutter*

Charles R. Hulten *Urban Institute*

Gerald D. Isaac *General Motors Corporation*

Gordon O. F. Johnson *LogEtronics*

Donald W. Kiefer *Library of Congress*

William Kitt *Eaton Corporation*

Jerome Kurtz *Paul, Weiss, Rifkind, Wharton & Garrison*

Roland L. Laing *Financial Executives Research Foundation*

Michael E. Levy *Conference Board*

F. Peter Libassi *Travelers Insurance Company*

Donald C. Lubick *Hodgson, Russ, Andrews, Woods & Goodyear*

Bruce K. MacLaury *Brookings Institution*

Martin G. Mand *E. I. du Pont de Nemours and Company*

Phillip L. Mann *Miller & Chevalier*

Rosemary Marcuss *Congressional Budget Office*

Samuel L. Maury *Business Roundtable*

Mark McConaghy *Price Waterhouse and Company*

Charles E. McLure, Jr. *Department of the Treasury*

Joseph J. Minarik *Urban Institute*

John S. Nolan *Miller & Chevalier*

R. Wayne Oates *PPG Industries*

Van Doorn Ooms *House Committee on the Budget*

Joseph A. Pechman *Brookings Institution*

Henry C. Ruempler *Citibank*

Michael P. Sampson *American University*

Robert B. Scharlotte *Goodyear Tire & Rubber Company*

Frank W. Schiff *Committee for Economic Development*

Garry J. Schinasi *Senate Committee on the Budget*

Joseph A. Sciarrino *Financial Executives Institute*

Bernard M. Shapiro *Price Waterhouse and Company*

Jennings T. Smith *Exxon Corporation*

John B. Spring *National Car Rental System*

C. Eugene Steuerle *Department of the Treasury*

Emil M. Sunley *Deloitte Haskins & Sells*

Vito Tanzi *International Monetary Fund*

Margo Thorning *American Council for Capital Formation*

Eric J. Toder *Department of the Treasury*

Thomas A. Troyer *Caplin & Drysdale*

Norman B. Ture *Institute for Research on the Economics of Taxation*

St. Clair J. Tweedie *American Cyanamid Company*

H. Stewart VanScoyoc *Charls E. Walker Associates*

James M. Verdier *Harvard University*

Elsie M. Watters *Tax Foundation*

Clifford H. Whitcomb *Prudential Property & Casualty Insurance Company*

John G. Wilkins *Department of the Treasury*